The Girl who Loved Mountains

The Girl who Loved Mountains

Frances Ridley Havergal

Lucille Travis

CF4·K

10 9 8 7 6 5 4 3 2 1
© Copyright 2014 Lucille Travis
Paperback ISBN 978-1-78191-522-6
epub ISBN 978-1-78191-532-5
mobi ISBN 978-1-78191-535-6

Published by Christian Focus Publications,
Geanies House, Fearn, Tain, Ross-shire,
IV20 1TW, Scotland, U.K.
Tel: +44 (0)1862 871011
Fax: +44 (0)1862 871699
www.christianfocus.com
email: info@christianfocus.com

Cover design by Daniel van Straaten
Cover illustration by Jeff Anderson
Printed and bound in Denmark by Nørhaven

Scripture quotations are taken from the King James
Version of the Bible (KJV).

Contents

Little Quicksilver 7

The Terrible Sermon 15

'I Fear You Are Not Prepared' 23

Can You Trust Jesus? 29

'You Must Not Go Back to School' 35

Alone in a Hard Place 43

Mission to Ireland 53

The New Governess 59

The Mountains of her Dreams 69

The Queen is Pleased 79

A Sudden Sorrow 87

In the Alps Again! 97

Full Surrender 109

'Kept' 121

God's Half-Timer 131

Faster Home 145

Thinking Further Topics 158

Frances Ridley Havergal Timeline 168

Bibliography 170

Author's Note 171

Old Recipe for Apple Turnover 172

Easy Recipe for Apple Turnover 173

To Shauna, a gift from God to all
who know her,
May the beautiful song of your heart
sound from every mountain top and
valley on your path.

Little Quicksilver

Everywhere great crowds of people were gathering for the coronation of the young Queen Victoria at Westminster Abbey. Shops were closed, houses empty as throngs filled the streets of London and cities, towns and villages all over the United Kingdom. It was the 28th of June, 1838 and in the rural parish of Astley the bell in the church tower had rung in the early morning to call the people together. A coronation of a young queen was quite a celebration. Tables piled with great joints of beef, loaves of bread and sweets of many kinds were set near the church wall next to a huge barrel of cider. Nearby friends and family stood, including young Frances Ridley Havergal, the newest addition to the rector of Astley's family. The crowd quietened as the rector raised his hands. When he began to sing in his fine voice, *God Save the Queen*, the crowds joined their voices to his, and behind him young Henry, his oldest son, lifted one-and-a-half-year-old Frances onto his shoulders, saying, 'You must sing too, and one day I will tell you how you welcomed the Queen this day.' And sing she did, though in her own way!

Some months later, when her second birthday came, Frances, now mostly called Fanny by the family, did know how to sing. At two years old, she spoke clearly and was learning faster than anyone could have imagined. But punctuality was not Fanny's strong suit and never would be. It was something, though, that her father held in high importance.

So when the bell had already rung calling the family together for morning prayers, Fanny should have paid attention but didn't. It was the 14th of December and outside the tall parlour window snow was falling. In the distance the hills looked blue-white. Her father's great, tall fir tree had soft white along its branches. Her mother's gardens below and the woods beyond were covered in snow. Fanny had climbed onto a chair to see and would not be moved, not even by her brother Frank who tugged at her to come down. 'But look, it's snowing,' she cried. 'It's snowing on my birthday.' She clapped her hands.

'You must come now, Fanny.' Frank said. 'Papa is waiting for you. Everyone else is ready to begin.' Taking one more long look, she stamped her small foot before she slid down from the chair and followed her brother.

'Come now, Fanny, even my favourite two-year-old girl must learn to be punctual.' Her father sat by the fireside and held out his arms to Fanny who ran into them.

'But Papa, it's snowing! It's snowing on my birthday,' she said, climbing onto his knees, a place reserved for the youngest.

'Your birthday! So it is,' her father said, nuzzling into the pile of light golden curls that covered her head till she giggled. 'But you, my little Quicksilver, must learn not to keep your mother and your sisters and brothers waiting.' From his pocket her father took out his large gold watch. 'Now, can you tell me what time it is?' Fanny's blue eyes shone with merriment. Her father loved clocks and they were everywhere in the house. Even the front of the church had a great clock that he had donated to the congregation.

She looked at the watch, giggled, and said. 'Yes, Papa, we always begin prayer time at 9 o'clock.'

'And then how late are you, child?' Her father was no longer smiling.

'I am very late,' she said softly. 'Maria has been teaching me to tell the time, and so I am five minutes late.'

Patting her head gently, her father, his face still unsmiling, looked around at the family and the servants, and asked, 'I shall abide by your judgement. Seeing as how it is her birthday, is it your will that we shall forgive her this time?' Laughter filled the room along with hearty 'yeses'.

'Then we shall indeed,' her pastor father said. 'Only remember, Fanny, that in this household, punctuality is the rule, and we must all hold fast to it. Now, shall we sing our thanks to the Lord for this fine snowy day?' In his rich and beautiful voice, her father began a hymn all of them knew, even Fanny. Her oldest sister, Miriam, had told her that when she was a baby, she cooed in time with the nursery rhymes her brother Frank, two years older than she, had sung to her.

'This is a singing household,' Miriam had said. 'Papa got his first gold medal for his beautiful hymn at the same time you were born.' Fanny had seen the shiny medal, and knew the beautiful hymn sung in English churches everywhere. 'And did you know that every Havergal child has gone to music school, just like you, first in the arms and on the shoulders of Papa?' Fanny had giggled. She did enjoy sitting on her father's shoulders when he played the harmonium, and she was learning to sing with him.

Her father also demanded punctuality, and her mother believed in activity and learning and resourcefulness. It was her mother, with her gentle ways, who had taught them all to read and write before they were old enough for school. Now, Miriam, home from school, had charge of two-year-old Fanny's half-hour lessons. By the time Fanny was three, she could read easy books, write in round hand[1], repeat her daily verses and sew patchwork stitches. At four years old, she could read harder books including the Bible. Her mother also taught the girls to sew for themselves and others, how to bake the famous 'Astley apple turnovers'[2] and how to help care for the sick and the poor in the small cottages nearby. Visiting with her mother was part of their training and Fanny learned to help carry the buckets of soup her mother often took to the needy among them. Her father also took them on his visits to the cottages.

---

1. A type of handwriting and calligraphy originating in England in the 1660s.

2 See recipe on page 172.

Fanny was four years old when her father took her with him to a cottage where a boy her own age had died. 'He died,' Papa explained, 'but he is now in heaven with Jesus.' The boy looked pale and quiet in his coffin, and Fanny wondered why he lay so still even when she lightly touched his cold hand. She said nothing and afterwards when her dog Flora, a small brown and white spaniel, came running to greet her at the garden gate, she quickly forgot about the boy.

On a visit with her sister Ellen to her grandmother and grandfather's house, it was almost the same when a letter came from her mother to tell her that one of the cottage babies had died.

Her mother wrote:

I am so glad to hear how happy you are at Wycombe ... I miss you and often think I hear you call "Mama", or expect you are coming to me. You remember the three little babies at Dunley. Jane, the one that you nursed, is gone to heaven. May my Fanny know and love Jesus Christ! Then she will be sure to go to heaven whether she dies young or old. Some of the seeds are come up in your garden; I love to watch them, because you helped me to sow them. Dear Papa sends his love. Goodbye, dear Fanny ...

Fanny thought of the baby, Jane, for a second and wondered if she too had been cold like the dead boy, but she hadn't a thought about heaven. True to her father's nickname for her, 'little Quicksilver', her mind turned straight away to the happy picture of her seeds in her mother's garden and she ran to tell her grandmother.

Back at Astley, she was free to run everywhere and explore the large grounds of the rectory, fields, gardens, the woods around the parsonage, and the little brook that ran through. Fanny and Flora had many daring adventures together.

One day, Fanny heard of a visiting Irish boy who had discovered two adders under the steep bank near the brook. He had caught them by the back of their necks and brought them to her father. The possibility of serpents and snakes made her adventures to the secluded brook all the more exciting. A rustle of leaves and the gleam of what might have been small dark eyes deep in a crevice of the bank made her sure there might be adders there still. 'We must go no closer, Flora,' she would whisper pointing to the bank. Flora's short sharp barks were enough to keep any adders away. 'We'll cross the brook further down on the old plank,' Fanny whispered to faithful Flora.

The trees she climbed were too high … the consequences being slips, falls, torn knees, scraped arms and severely torn stockings could not be hidden. Her sisters shook their heads and gave her lectures along with bandages, but she could never be sorry for more than a moment and was soon laughing and on to the next adventure. It was Flora who knew her plans to be a poet and probably a mountain climber too. But there was another side to Frances Ridley Havergal, and it was beginning to show!

From the first day that she had hidden behind a thick window drape in the upstairs hallway to eavesdrop on the German tutor, Mr. Lowes, Fanny found herself learning German along with her brothers and sisters. How easily it came to her as she quietly repeated the lessons to herself. One day, Mr. Lowes discovered her standing in the hallway pressed against the wall just outside the door to the classroom. 'Good morning, Miss Frances. Were you wanting something?' he said. She answered him in perfect German. An astonished Mr. Lowes reported his discovery and begged that she be allowed to take lessons with the others.

'She is so young,' her mother said. 'We will need to be careful that she does not overtax her mind.'

'Yes, my dear, but our little Quicksilver will be better off sitting inside the schoolroom learning German than standing in the hallway learning it.' Her father laughed and held out his hand to Mr. Lowes. 'It seems you are to have a new pupil, sir.' It was to be only the first of many new things for Fanny. French and music would soon follow. Fanny loved to learn and advanced quickly beyond her age. However, even Fanny would soon forget her studies for a while. Her sister Miriam was going to marry Henry Crane in October! And not only that, but the Havergal family was leaving Astley for the new Rectory of St. Nicholas in the city of Worcester.

First they would go to stay at Henwick House near the village of Hallow for a while. Fanny danced with joy at the exciting news. 'You will have fields and gardens and trees to roam,' her father promised. 'I believe Henwick will be all that my little Quicksilver could wish for.'

'Yes, Papa. We will love our new house, but what shall we do with Flora at the wedding?'

Her father laughed and patted her head. 'Someone will look after her while we are gone.' Fanny dreamed of the new adventures to come in the countryside at Henwick. She could hardly wait for Miriam's wedding. Miriam, dark-haired and dark-eyed like their father, looked like a princess in her gown of pale-blue satin with lace embroidery and her crown of flowers. It was Fanny's first wedding and so beautiful, Fanny knew she would never forget it.

Henwick House at Hallow was all that her father had promised. Fanny threw herself into the new surroundings with all its wonderful wildness, and Flora followed at her heels. She didn't notice the change in poor Flora until it was too late. One morning, Flora did not come to greet her. The little dog lay still and cold in her basket.

'I'm afraid Flora is dead,' her father explained.

Tears streamed down Fanny's face.

'It is her first sorrow,' her mother whispered as later that day the family stood by the white blooming Mespilus tree in the back garden where Flora lay buried. Fanny had written a paper to mark the spot:

Here lies little Flora,
Died 16th, April 1844,
Aged 7, Reverence her remains.

Fanny could not imagine the other changes that were soon to come.

The Terrible Sermon

Fanny, like her nickname Quicksilver, could never be still long and whatever came next took all her attention. Flora soon became a distant memory and the pain began to ease. The morning bell still sounded, and her father's clocks kept the time in their new house. Her father's music, and mother's cheerful ways made it seem to Fanny as if almost nothing had changed. And the trees and stone walls at Henwick still needed to be climbed, the always changing fields explored and her new books read.

'You are the merriest, most thoughtless, determined little sister ever I saw.'

Ellen, fair-haired like their mother, and like her in so many ways, was just as determined that Fanny would learn all she needed to learn. She firmly scolded Fanny now as she bandaged the little girl's knee. 'These stockings will have to be mended again, and one day it will be you mending them.' With a gentle hand she finished tying the small bandage in place. 'Fanny, dear, you are six years old, and it's time you asked dear Jesus to help you do better. Will you pray with me?'

Ellen had their mother's blonde hair, but their father's dark eyes, and like their father's, they sometimes seemed to be seeing something inside her, but Fanny couldn't think what it might be. She had no intention of praying with Ellen. She had no time, nor any need at all. 'I think I must go upstairs and rest my knee, Ellen,' she said. She didn't say that her latest book lay upstairs hidden under a table where she would soon be too.

Sunday dawned clear and cool, and the horses were neighing impatiently by the time the family were all in place for the drive to Hallow Church near Worcester to hear a sermon preached by a Mr. Philpotts. The country church was filled. Fanny sat with Ellen on one side and Maria on the other, a good thing since she loved to sing the church songs with them. When it was time for the sermon, Mr. Philpotts stood in the pulpit; a tall, dark haired man, who looked very solemn and even taller in his long black robe and vestments. Fanny sat up straight and still, not wanting to miss a single word, as he announced his sermon this morning would be on hell!

No one could have missed a word of this preacher, especially not Fanny as she listened to him tell of hell's terrors pictured in all its blazing judgement on all the sinners there. 'If you are an unrepentant sinner here this morning, I urge you to listen carefully,' he said. Fanny held her breath. 'Hear the words of Jonathan Edwards's sermon, *Sinners in the Hands of an Angry God:*

'Sinners ... consider the fearful danger you are in,' he read, 'like a spider on a slender thread you hang from the hand of a holy God above the bottomless pit full of the fire of His wrath. It is nothing but His hand that holds you from falling into the fire every moment or that you did not go to hell last night, where there will be no end to its horrible misery for you, no end forever.' There was more, Bible texts about hell and judgement and Fanny couldn't help hearing every word. That night, haunting, fearful dreams came and she woke shivering, but she said nothing to anyone. If only the fearful words of Mr. Philpotts would go away she could be perfectly happy, but they began to come back to her more and more.

Fanny slipped quickly and as quietly as she could past the sewing room where Ellen was working on a quilt. Sure that Ellen was eager to pray with her, as her sisters always were, she heaved a sigh of relief when she was safely past. She didn't want to be read to from the Bible, or prayed with by those closest to her, and found every possible excuse not to let it happen. Though she hid it well, a feeling of unhappiness sprang up inside her. But as soon as her attention turned to some new interest she quickly forgot about all the rest. She decided that perhaps if she prayed and read the Bible by herself on Sunday afternoons it would make her feel better, and for a while she tried it.

On a quiet Sunday afternoon, when no one in the family was around to see her, she went into a small upstairs room and carefully closed the door behind her. First she would read a chapter in the New Testament. Fanny had read the Bible at four and now read with ease.

Finished, she knelt down to pray a little. 'There, I think I feel happier already,' she said. Her Sunday afternoon trips to the upstairs room were fairly frequent, though she gave them no thought at all the rest of the week. One Sunday afternoon, Marion, a girl her own age, was visiting. Fanny decided she would not let that stand in the way of her Sunday ritual. She would just have to include Marion.

'Marion,' she said, 'If you like, I will share a secret with you, but you must promise to tell no one.'

Marion's dark eyes grew wide. 'Oh, Fanny, I love nothing better than a secret. I do promise no one else shall know of it from me.' Fanny nodded, then putting a finger to her lips to warn they must be quiet, she led the way upstairs to the front room. Once safely inside it, she gave Marion a conspirator's hug.

'This,' said Francis, 'is my very own little church. I come here every Sunday and never miss. Since you are my dear guest today, what else could I do but bring you with me?' Marion was speechless as she looked around at the spare little room and nodded. Taking Marion's arm, Fanny said, 'Shall we kneel together, and I will pray?'

Fanny's prayer was quite short and simple. 'There now,' she said. 'I don't think I will read a chapter from the New Testament today, since we have so little time left to spend together. I know Mama has a special tea planned for us.' At the door, Fanny again pressed her finger to her lips. 'Remember, no one else must know the secret or I may not be allowed to come up here alone every Sunday.' Her words were not exactly true! If her sisters or anyone in the family had known of her Sunday afternoon routine, they would have been glad of it. But Fanny knew that the discovery of this activity would lead to a whole lot more questions!

Marion's face was full of sympathy. 'Oh, I promise, Fanny, that I will never tell anyone. You will not be forbidden such devotion on my account.'

Fanny nodded. She couldn't help herself, but she was almost enjoying Marion's vow of silence. 'What's done is done,' her heart whispered. Maybe she wouldn't even see Marion again. It was possible since they were already packing to leave for her father's next church assignment at St. Nicholas.

Most nights Fanny didn't pray, but this week spring had come and breathed fresh, sweet green on all the trees and the gardens at Henwick. The sun was shining, the sky was blue, and Fanny could feel it all deep inside her. Sitting under a tree with the sun peeping through a leafy hole above seemed to touch her with such warm wonder and joy inside, almost the way listening to splendid music did. This morning her father had reminded the family of lines from the poet Cowper: 'My Father made them all.' And this made her think of how truly happy she would be if she could say the same words and mean them. If only God would make her a Christian before summer came, she would enjoy his works so much better! Instead of praying, Fanny sighed.

'I am not a Christian and probably I will not be. I am so naughty and I can't help liking it sometimes. God would not want me anyway.' But when spring days and soft evenings came in full, she felt overwhelmed with their beauty and the words of Cowper's poem came back to tease her. They were there waiting to come to her mind whenever she saw a lovely scene letting her know she was missing something she couldn't have because she was not a Christian. Soon enough there would be no tall trees waiting to shelter her, no small grave where her dog Flora lay buried, no green fields stretching as far as she could see, no hills and forest, no wild flowers; they were leaving the countryside! Fanny could feel the great bitterness of her loss deep inside her.

The large Rectory of St. Nicholas was next to the church in the city of Worcester. Fanny now had her own tiny room. Her mother did her best to make the room bright with white curtains and pink edging. 'Fanny, this is your own room and I pray it will be your Bethel.' Fanny didn't ask her what she meant, but she would soon come to find her little bedroom a place of escape into a whole new world.

Only her father, who loved the trees and gardens he had planted and left behind at Astley, knew how much Fanny mourned her loss of these things now. After several weeks at St. Nicholas, her father pulled her close into his big arms and whispered. 'You are like a caged lark, daughter. I know you miss running free at Henwick, but I am waiting for the day to come when the songs come back to your heart. They will, child, they will. You must sing with your father, mother and family. Then one day you will hear the music again coming from inside.' Fanny swallowed hard. She did feel like a caged lark. It was the window in her small room that showed her a whole new world she could freely enter.

The day was clear, and great white clouds filled the blue sky like mountains waiting to be climbed. Since she'd read her first books about mountains, Fanny had longed to climb them. Pictures of the great Swiss Alps with snow-topped peaks, huge jagged-edged rocks that dared a climber to attempt them filled her with joy and a burning desire to try. As she stared at the clouds in her upstairs window, she imagined climbing to their heights. It was a game she could play any time and she did. They were never the same for long and she loved each new shape and challenge. She read everything she could find on mountains.

Sadly, one day she read about the clouds only to discover they were vapours one could never climb. The clouds she loved to pretend climbing became what they really were: clouds. However, one day she would climb the real mountains with their snow tops. She knew she would, knew she must climb those mountains where the snow was so pure and white.

One morning, her father said, 'Here is something that might cheer you. Shall we play a little game?' His voice had laughter in it, the teasing kind. 'I will only tell you that the curate who is coming to preach next Sunday is one of your favourite preachers. He is not tall or short, fat or thin, and I do not recall the colour of his eyes. Now, who might it be?' Fanny laughed and began to guess, but finally her father held up his hand and exclaimed, 'Enough! Since you have so many favourites, you will just have to wait and see.'

Sunday came and Fanny could hardly wait to see the visiting curate. Unfortunately, the curate who was to visit, a preacher she did know and enjoy, was home with a bad throat. The curate who took his place, preached a sermon called, *Fear not, little flock*. Fanny longed to talk about her fears to him. When an opportunity came, Fanny found herself telling this man her heart's troubles. His advice fell on her ears and into her heart like a dry, scratching wind on thirsty ground. 'You have nothing to fear, child,' he said, 'it's the excitement of moving, and all these new scenes that are making you feel so, and it will soon go off. You must try and be a good girl and pray.' Fanny was spared any more by the dinner bell. Only one thing was certain: she would never speak of her fears to anyone again.

That night, she tried to think about God. 'It was very nice that Jesus died for our sins,' she whispered. She tried to be sorry, tried to believe, but she didn't believe it was for her, and the only tears that came spilled from her frustration, her anger that she needed a happy heart and quickly, but could not get it at all.

'I Fear You Are Not Prepared'

Fanny pulled on a shawl and picked up the basket of small clothes and soft blankets she and Maria were taking to a mother with a new baby. Fanny tucked in a tiny cap she had knitted for the little one. Maria had taught her to knit and now that she was ten she loved knitting caps for the babies. Maria carried a bucket of soup and a basket of fresh rolls and jams. 'Let me help you with the soup,' Fanny offered.

'That will be fine. We do make a good team these days.' Maria slid her hand to one side of the bucket handles so Fanny could grip it too. Maria frowned slightly. 'I only wish Mama had been well enough to come with us today. She is so good with the mothers and children.'

'You'll do just fine,' Fanny said and laughed. Of all her sisters, Maria was always the one off on a visit to the almshouse poor, the Sunday school, children's homes, mission meetings, wherever there was something she could do to help. Fanny loved her sister dearly. If only Maria was not so eager to catch Fanny in conversations about God. She might even try to pray with Fanny as they walked. Fanny was relieved that they were soon at the small home.

When they entered the little cottage, it was bursting with a family of eight children and a ninth now in its mother's arms. While Maria tended the mother and her new baby, Fanny asked the oldest, a girl named Anna who attended her Sunday school class, to help settle the younger ones for a promised hot roll and a story. 'Will you sing us one of the Sunday school songs, Miss? You do sing ever so pretty,' Anna asked.

Fanny sat on a low stool surrounded by the children, their hands already reaching out for a roll. She sang not one but two songs, and by then the children were licking the last crumbs from sticky fingers. 'Come now,' she said, 'let's sing together.' Lifting the smallest, a toddler with a very sticky face, onto her lap, Fanny began to sing, *Twinkle, Twinkle Little Star* and soon the children were singing with her. 'Very good,' Fanny said, 'and when we come again I shall teach you some new words to that song, if you like.'

'Oh yes, Miss, please,' a girl of about six begged. Fanny giggled as she heard a younger brother whisper loudly, 'She be bringing more rolls too?' Just then, Maria, who never missed an opportunity for a Bible reading, called for their attention.

The air felt cool, almost sharp when they left the cottage and Fanny pulled her thick shawl close about her. 'The weather has turned a bit,' Maria said, 'I'm glad Mama did not try to come out today, she looked a bit pale this morning. She would have loved to see you with the little ones. I think you will like coming back to teach them Papa's beautiful song.' It was a song their father had written to the tune of *Twinkle, Twinkle Little Star*.

'Well,' Fanny agreed, 'the children did seem to like singing, though I'm sure they liked the jam and rolls even more.' She laughed happily. But on Sunday, Fanny noticed something that made her feel sad and suddenly determined. The day was cold enough so that the Sunday school room felt cool in spite of Fanny's thick, green wool dress and matching jacket. She made a point of smiling at Anna, the girl from the cottage she and Maria had visited. The girl shyly smiled back then hurried to sit with her classmates. Fanny noticed Anna kept her thin shawl on, worn as it was. Looking around, she began to notice how many of the other cottage children wore clothes that were too thin for such weather; worn skirts, ragged shawls or threadbare jackets. She was sure it was all they had. She thought about her own warm clothes. Thanks to her mother all the Havergal girls had good, serviceable clothing and the occasional elegant dress when needed. Fanny began to think of a plan.

'Mama, we must help them.' Fanny and her friend Sarah had come up with an idea to help provide clothes for needy children in the Sunday school class. 'We can take subscriptions each month from August to October. Our friends may give any amount from three pence to one shilling to 'The Flannel Petticoat Society' for the clothing of these children.

'Yes,' said Sarah, who looked as eager as Fanny. 'And we so much want you, Mrs. Havergal, to be our chief adviser on shopping and dressmaking."

'Maria and Ellen have already said they would be glad to select the children,' Fanny added. Her mother was smiling, and so 'The Flannel Petticoat Society' began.

The 5th of November became the day that between twenty-five and thirty children were invited to the rectory to receive new clothes. The house was decorated, and Fanny felt a thrill of pride go through her as the children came. After exchanging their old rags for well-fitted new clothing, a celebration followed with hymn singing and cake for all. The work, the excitement, and the feeling of doing a kindness did make Fanny feel better inside, the same way she felt on visits with Maria to the poor in the almshouse, or singing at the annual holiday party for them. But underneath she knew she was not a Christian and had less and less hope of becoming one.

Then there was some bad news. Her mother was sick. Fanny could see how pale she looked even though her eyes brightened when Fanny came to sit by her bedside. 'Mama is very ill,' Maria had told her, but Fanny didn't really listen to her, or any of the family.

'Mama dear, you will be better soon and can go to church again.'

'I will be going to the true church, child, in heaven.' As her mother held Fanny's hand in her own, she said,

'Fanny, you are my youngest, and I am concerned most for you, child. Fanny dear, pray to God to prepare you for all that he is preparing for you.' Her mother tired quickly and Fanny left her sleeping. Fanny thought of her mother's words and hoped God might be preparing a mansion for her, but she didn't think so. How could that be when she so often felt naughty? It was July now, and already Fanny was eleven years old, and thinking and planning for her next December birthday. With one last glimpse of her sleeping mother, she closed the door softly, and quickly forgot her mother's words to her, the last words she would ever hear her say.

When her father gently told her that her mother was dead, Fanny could not accept the truth. Again and again when no one was near to see her, she slipped into the darkened room where her beautiful mother lay so still and peaceful. She had heard of people who'd only been in a stupor and were not dead at all, perhaps her mother would wake up any time now. But each time she lifted the curtain to see her mother's face there was no change at all.

On the day of the funeral, Fanny watched the funeral procession from her window and knew at last her terrible loss. Her dear mother was gone and Fanny's heart broke. Alone in her room, she wept until she fell asleep. But like all the sorrows and longings hidden deep inside, this one too she hid from all around her, and it seemed to others as if she had quickly recovered from her mother's death.

Her father took them all to Wales for a visit, and when they returned, Fanny visited her married sister at Oakhampton. Fanny, true to her old nickname Quicksilver, soon threw herself into whatever caught her attention. She laughed easily, once again her old free-spirited, strong-willed self, carefree to the point of leaving her writing journals and books wherever she'd put them down. 'She is a bit of trouble,' Miriam would say, 'but so appreciative of any treats and ready to be merry.'

What no one knew were the nights when Fanny lay in bed trying to think about God, frightened of him, but determined. Lying in bed, Fanny would begin with a half-whisper, 'How good of God to send Jesus to die!' She said the words but didn't feel them, certainly she didn't feel his goodness at all. She didn't, couldn't love God for his goodness, and it made her feel a mixture of fear and anger and wanting what she didn't have. Often she ended the night crying into her pillow.

It was August, 1850 and Fanny, aged thirteen, was to go off to an exclusive boarding school. She could hardly wait! The night before she was to leave, Ellen sat brushing her hair gently. 'Fanny, you are entering a new chapter in your life,' she said. Fanny waited quietly for what she knew was coming. Ellen went on to talk about God's love, and how good it was to love him, until Fanny could not bear it.

She decided to break her silence. 'I can't love God yet, Ellen,' she said. She wanted to say more but couldn't. In the morning, it was Maria who took her on the day's journey to school.

Can You Trust Jesus?

Fanny and Maria arrived at the Belmont School near London late in the evening. The two were welcomed and served tea in the large drawing room while they waited for chapel to be over. They had finished tea when they heard singing and Fanny urged Maria to come with her to listen. Miss Teed, the principal, came quickly to invite them in. Fanny was too tired and excited to remember much of the evening talk, but one thing stuck in her mind. The speaker had urged them to begin the school term with the Saviour who loved us and gave himself for us. For the first time, Fanny knelt next to her small, white, curtain-less school bed. 'Oh to believe in Jesus, to believe that he has pardoned me,' she whispered. On the outside she was still merry and light-hearted as before, but deep inside her was a sad emptiness she knew only the faith she did not have could fill. Weeks ago, she had begun reading the Bible straight through, determined that if eternal life was in there she would find it. Her hope was that here at Belmont school, things would change.

Fanny quickly made friends, among them a dark-haired, energetic classmate named Elizabeth Clay. Both girls shared so much in common that the two soon became close friends. Fanny knew that many of the students were Christians, including Elizabeth and another close friend, Mary. Miss Teed and her teachers were committed Christians, kind and competent at their jobs. As always, Fanny excelled in her studies. She had been well prepared at home, even for the rule at Belmont that all must speak only in French. But as the weeks passed, she longed to share the unhappiness inside her with someone. One day, as she walked in the garden with Mary, it happened. Like the close friend she had become, Mary poured out loving sympathy and comfort.

'Oh Fanny, I know that Jesus' love is for you too. Remember how he spoke of letting the children come to him.' Mary quoted many Scriptures, all of them refreshing to Fanny's heart. Again and again they found time to talk, and Fanny was now certain that only Christ could satisfy her. Over and over she prayed, at night, and during the day if she was alone, but she had not yet heard any voice, or any answer.

Another of her classmates, Diana, was the most gentle, kindest and loving of them all. Fanny was certain that Diana was a Christian. She could not bring herself to open her heart to Diana the way she did with Mary, but how she wished she could. The term was flying by, already December, and for several days Fanny had noticed a quietness in Diana, almost a sadness in her manner like depression. Today, she hadn't seen her at all.

That evening at tea, Fanny, sitting across from Diana, saw the most remarkable thing! Diana's face looked so bright and her voice had a new sound, a gladness in everything she said.

Diana sat down next to Fanny and threw her arm around her, saying words that amazed her! 'Oh Fanny, dearest Fanny, the blessing has come to me at last. Jesus has forgiven me, I know. He is my Saviour, and I am so happy! Only come to him, Fanny, and he will receive you. You know that everyone thought I was a Christian, but I wasn't. Oh Fanny, I wasn't a Christian until the moment his words, "Your sins are forgiven you," suddenly struck me, and I believed they were for me. I believed that he loved me, and his death was for my pardon. Before that, I tried to do all the right things, but my motives were not right. I can hardly tell you how changed things seem now. Fanny, my heart is full of joy and everything seems new.'

Tears filled Fanny's eyes as she hugged Diana and said, 'Oh Diana, I am so glad for you.' Fanny was awestruck. 'I'm so happy for you, really,' she said again. The chapel bell was calling them for evening prayers, and Fanny, glad for the escape, said no more; she couldn't have. She longed for what had come to Diana, and despaired of ever having it.

The final weeks of the term came to a close, and Fanny was glad. December holidays and her birthday lay ahead, just what she needed. She couldn't wait to see her father's face, feel his loving hug, hear his deep voice leading the family in song. There would also be the longed-for visits to Miriam's house. Outside, it was snowing as Fanny waved goodbye to Mary and Elizabeth and ran to the carriage where Maria stood waiting for her. On a sudden impulse she stopped, scooped up a handful of snow and threw it to Maria, laughing as her surprised sister wiped snow from her face and jacket.

Maria hugged her close, wet jacket and all. 'You haven't changed, little sister,' she said. 'You are as merry and as thoughtless as ever.' Fanny laughed again, hoping that the ride home would be a cheerful one, and that Maria would not try to talk about God on the way. She had nothing to say that Maria or any of the family would want to hear, not yet.

Fanny loved going to her sister Miriam's home at Oakhampton in the countryside. The fields and woods, the gardens so like the ones she'd loved at Astley were like a tonic to her heart. Inside the great home, even Oakhampton's parlour and dining room, its halls and its large fireplace mantels were draped with sweet-smelling evergreen branches and red berries for the Christmas season. Miriam had invited friends as well as the family and the house was filled with activity. Miss Caroline Cooke was one of the guests, the kind of person that Fanny immediately felt at home with. Fanny often found her sitting alone by the fire in a small room near the parlour, knitting in the lull between early evening and supper. 'Come, sit with me, Fanny, I hoped you might turn up to help me enjoy this lovely fire.' Fanny liked Miss Cooke's company, the way she listened when they talked and the sort of things she said.

She was dark-haired, a pretty woman about father's age, Fanny thought. A good and godly woman too. Soon Fanny began to talk with her of things she'd only been able to talk about with her schoolmate, Mary.

Late one afternoon, as shadows touched the corners of the little sitting room where she sat with Miss Cooke, the soft light of the oil lamps and the glow of the firelight that rose and fell seemed to warm Fanny's heart. And suddenly words frozen inside began to spill out. 'I would give everything I have to know that I am forgiven,' she said, 'even the love of my papa and family.'

For a moment Miss Cooke was still. 'Then,' she said, 'Fanny, I think, I am sure, it will not be very long before your desire is granted, your hope fulfilled.' Fanny listened to every word as Miss Cooke talked of Jesus and when she gently asked Fanny, 'Why can you not trust yourself to your Saviour at once?' Fanny's heart raced. 'If this moment Christ were to come in the clouds of heaven, and take up his redeemed, could you not trust him?' She said more, but a feeling of hope had flashed across Fanny, leaving her almost breathless!

'I could, surely,' she cried, and without another word Fanny ran from the sitting room and headed straight to her room, flung herself on her knees and at last knew she could trust the Lord Jesus, she did trust him. 'I do trust you, Lord Jesus and commit my soul to you,' she prayed. She knew that this was the faith she'd longed for, trusting the Lord Jesus, with her all, for eternity. She no longer needed to fear the Lord's coming, and happiness filled her so that even the room about her looked brighter. Joy had really come into her heart!

In the days that followed, Fanny loved what she read in her Bible each time she read it. The family was going to the nearby village of Bewdley in the large carriage, and Fanny chose to ride alone on the bench seat outside the carriage. She needed to finish reading the fourteenth chapter of John. She could do without the merriment and conversation inside the carriage, and there was no one up here to disturb her. The loving words of Jesus, his reminder not to be afraid, were like water for her thirsty heart. The ride to Bewdley was all too short.

Then the holiday celebrations were over and Miss Cooke was leaving. Fanny hugged her tight and whispered, 'I can never thank you enough for praying for me, listening to me, showing me the way. I do love you and will miss you.'

Miss Cooke's beautiful face seemed to glow as she looked down at Fanny. 'I do love you too, and perhaps it will not be long before we see each other again.'

Her father stood waiting to take Miss Cooke to the carriage. 'Yes,' he said, 'not long, but we really must go, Caroline, it's time.' Fanny smiled. Her punctual father was escorting Miss Cooke home. Fanny thought for a second that Miss Cooke blushed as her father took her arm. Had he really called Miss Cooke, Caroline?

'You Must Not Go Back
to School'

The rectory sewing room at St. Nicholas had never been so full of silks and satins and laces, and Fanny couldn't wait to see the final gown she would wear at the wedding; her own dear father's and Miss Cooke's wedding! 'You must hold still, Fanny,' Maria insisted, 'until this tuck is pinned. You are as slender as a reed. I only wish my own gown would need so many tucks. I am far too fond of apple turnovers.'

Fanny giggled, trying not to move as Maria pinned the bodice of her new dress. 'Maria, you are fond of lots of sweets, but on you they look just right. You will be the finest of bridesmaids and I will write a poem to tell it all, a wedding poem!'

Maria stepped back to see her work. 'Good!' she said. 'And, little sister, since you have been writing everything in rhyme from the age of seven, I am sure you will write a wedding poem. Stopping you would be like turning back the spring that used to run through Astley woods; you would spill out poems and leave them lying everywhere, as you did back then.'

Fanny laughed. 'Surely I am more careful now,' she said.

Maria smiled and then looked thoughtful. 'I suppose you are now that you are well into your fourteenth birthday, but things are about to change, Fanny. You will have a new mother and this will be her house too. We must think of her as our mother and help her all we can.' Fanny nodded. She already loved Miss Cooke, and the change would be good. If only now she would be more thoughtful of others. Sometimes the need inside to be the best at whatever she was doing drove her to forget everything else around her.

The wedding took Fanny's breath away. There was her beloved father, standing near the church altar, so tall and handsome in his dark wedding suit, smiling, and with eyes only for his new bride. Miss Cooke's soft, white veil floated about her and she looked like a princess in her silk dress etched with delicate lace. Fanny swallowed hard. She would have clapped for joy if she could have. The family, the guests, the grand wedding feast that followed, all of it was all Fanny could have dreamt of. Would she have a wedding of her own like this someday?

Her new mother was everything Fanny could have asked for, and the household soon filled with laughter and activity, and her father's punctuality! Fanny still read everything she could find to fill her appetite for learning. On the day that her father announced she could go to school at nearby Powick Court in Worcester, she clapped her hands for joy! She arrived at the school early on 5th August and was invited into the drawing room for tea, where she promptly threw her arms about an astonished principal, saying, 'Oh, I am so delighted to come to school!'

It was nearly December when Miss Haynes, the principal, took Fanny aside into her office for a word. Miss Hayne's face beamed. 'Fanny, I am so pleased to tell you that I've not only seen how intensely you keep to your studies, but I want you to know that you have excelled in them. You are well on your way to receiving some important honours.' Fanny left the office feeling even more determined to work harder than ever to finish well. She could hardly wait to write to Elizabeth to tell her the good news. Elizabeth wrote back, 'So glad for you, and I'll be praying! Can't wait either for the holidays, and Mama says "Yes" we will plan to visit you all.' Inside the envelope was a sketch Elizabeth had made of the gardens, the very ones Fanny had admired so much at Elizabeth's home last summer.

With just weeks to go to finish the term, Fanny had gone to bed feeling more tired than she'd ever felt. Her face even hurt. By morning, she could hardly see through eyes almost swollen shut. Her head ached and though she heard the doctor's voice saying, 'We must send you home, child, until you are well again,' she was too sick to care. Her father had come to carry her out into the waiting carriage. Her mother's soothing voice was the last thing Fanny heard until she awoke back in her own bed. The doctor came often that first week.

'Severe erysipelas[1] in her face and head,' he said. 'She must have complete rest and nourishing food as soon as she can take it. I fear it will be many weeks before this young lady is up and about.'

Fanny's whole body ached, especially her head and swollen face. Worse, she was almost blind! For many weeks, Fanny had to lie still. Maria sat by her bedside each day taking turns with her mother reading the Bible to her, sometimes talking, even singing verses of Fanny's favourite hymns. It was her father's visits that she loved most. She must lie still and quiet, doctor's orders, and her father knew how hard it was for his Quicksilver daughter to be still at all.

As the weeks passed, the hot swelling of her face lessened. Her eyes burned and headaches came suddenly, but she was healing and becoming restless. Letters from Elizabeth, though she loved listening to her talk about school life, made her wonder if she would ever catch up with her classes. When she was finally allowed to get up, Fanny's heart sank when she was told, 'There must be no more school, not even studying at home! It will take months yet for your full recovery.'

By winter's end, Fanny's eyes were better and her headaches gone. By the end of June, she and Maria were taking walks together. One day, Maria guided them to a small park with a little stream to see the new duckling families. They were standing watching four little ducklings swimming after their mother, when

---

1. An acute disease of the skin, with fever and raised purplish patches.

Maria gently turned Fanny's face to look at her. 'Now, Fanny, before we go one step farther, and before I burst from keeping good news from you, I must tell you. Papa is taking us to Wales.' Fanny was speechless. Maria smiled. 'You know, dear, that Papa's eyes have bothered him more lately, and the rest will do him good. Papa thinks you are well enough to travel, and Doctor Tolley agrees. So, little sister, while we are off walking, Mama is packing your things. Ellen and Frank are coming too. We leave for Wales the day after tomorrow. Unless, of course, you don't want to go,' she teased.

Fanny hugged her. 'Oh, if you left me at home I think I could not last a day,' she cried. She couldn't wait to be off to Wales, or anywhere!

Fanny loved the town of Llandudno in North Wales between the Welsh mainland and the great Orme peninsula, a limestone headland that rose high above. Copper mines had been dug deep into the Orme's Head, and Fanny wondered what it would be like to be half a mile down from daylight. Surely Ellen and Frank would want to know too. Frank finally gave in and hired a mine truck and a guide to take them. That evening when the miners had left, the three of them piled into the little truck and were pushed half a mile down, till they could only see daylight as a tiny star above them. Fanny felt the darkness, the deep silence and the chilly air. 'Follow me closely,' the guide said as he led them through the mine into strange caverns, some full of crystals and copper ore. Fanny had never seen or felt anything like it. 'If only Elizabeth could see this,' she whispered. She would try to share it all in a letter.

It was weeks before Fanny sat down to write her letter to Elizabeth. She wrote first about the wonders of the copper mine, but it had been a full month since, and there was so much more to tell.

> *Oh, Elizabeth, we've gone on so many walks. I like best to explore alone and I can hardly tell you of the breakneck places and precipices here that I find myself among. I am almost too venturesome, but my foot has never once slipped. Then too, in such wild places I am quite alone, and I take out my little Testament and read and pray where no human being besides myself is ever likely to be. Last week I couldn't do this, for I was very poorly from over-bathing in the sea and now I must not bathe. It is very annoying, for I like swimming and enjoy riding on the crested waves of the sea as much as on one of the wicked little ponies here.*
>
> *Oh, about W.H., I do hope when he goes back to school he will resist temptation! When I went to Powick last year I began prayerfully, but gradually I let the desire to surpass others in everything, my unwillingness to be behind, take over. I never can be content to be last … it is my besetting sin, pride, and it needs to go before the Lord can enter my heart.*

In August, the family went to lodgings in Colwyn, North Wales. The town of Colwyn was halfway along the north coast of Wales between the Irish Sea and the Pwllycrochen Woods on the towering hillside. Here, winds called 'the Foehn', that came from the south, crossed the nearby mountains warming Colwyn like few places in Wales. There were pretty walks everywhere. One could rent a donkey too, and a guide to go exploring. Fanny wrote to Elizabeth,

> *The change is doing us all good, and Papa's eyes are a little better. Colwyn suits me much better than Llandudno, and I am as well as possible. The donkey-girl (the donkeys for hire come with a girl or a boy to lead them about while one rides) teaches me Welsh. I think I learn it very fast, and I have a Welsh Testament and a Prayer Book. At what is called the 'Taffy service' where the traditional taffy-treacle coffee is served, I can sing and chant and respond as fully as the natives themselves.*
>
> *I wish I were not so impatient as I am, at hearing the (to me) dreadful news that I must on no account go to school again till after Christmas, and perhaps not at all! Still, I am sure it will be all right; and if I receive good things at the hand of the heavenly Father, I must not murmur at such a drawback, which is only to teach me a lesson I must learn after all … I have been thinking about my confirmation (at the Cathedral), though it will not be for two years. It seems such a solemn vow I fear I should never have strength to keep it. But it is one of my most constant prayers that, if I am spared to be confirmed, I may never act as if I had not been … I should so like to be confirmed with you …*

When it was time to leave for Worcester, Fanny watched as Ellen finished a small sketch of their Colwyn lodgings. 'It's good,' Fanny pronounced, 'and just in time. I see Papa waiting for us.'

But by November, it was clear to everyone that her father could no longer read from the church lectern. He decided to visit the well-known oculist, Dr. De Leuw in Grafrath, Germany. Fanny would go too.

'Incipient cataract,' the doctor announced. 'We shall try to disperse this, and perhaps we shall need no more than three weeks.' Grafrath had many nice walking places and Fanny was able to use her German everywhere she went. In a letter to Elizabeth she wrote:

> *Grafrath must be pretty in summer, and the hotel we are staying at is quaint. The master of our hotel, who likes cats and dogs, has so many it makes me laugh to hear them following him upstairs to bed each night, all fifty-two feet making a gentle patter on the stairs. We will be going to Düsseldorf for the winter, and at last I am allowed to go to school. I will tell you about my new school (how I long to go). The Luisenschule is called so after the Queen of Prussia. There are no private schools here, and all the young ladies seem to attend this school, 110 of them. Of course, everything will be in German, good practice for me ...*

Fanny loved a challenge, especially the school kind; what she didn't expect was the challenge of another kind that waited for her at Luisenschule.

Alone in a Hard Place

Fräulein Quincke, the schoolmistress, welcomed Fanny, the new Engländerin (English girl) and Fanny responded in the perfect German she had learned since childhood. She soon found her teachers very good. But there was one problem, a big one she couldn't escape or solve. In a school of 111 students, Fanny found herself the only Christian. Her fellow classmates cared nothing about religion and enjoyed making rude remarks about Christianity outside the classrooms. Worse, they were determined to make this sixteen-year-old English Christian girl as miserable as they could.

For the third time, Fanny found her bed rumpled, and a search beneath the covers revealed another mess of stale buttered bread, some crumbs still sticky with jelly. At least this time her Bible was still where she'd left it and not hidden in a cupboard or left lying in some empty classroom waiting for the janitor to find. Tricks like this were the least of her worries. No English school would have had so little supervision outside the classrooms, and Fanny faced far meaner things than crumbs in her bed. A girl called Olga was strong in every sport and well looked up to but she called Fanny by names Fanny would not repeat to anyone.

Olga saw to it that Fanny sat alone at socials. The other girls took Olga's lead and snubbed her, mocked her and seemed to enjoy the little things they could do to cause her trouble. Only when Fanny threw herself into her studies and her music lessons could she forget these troubles.

One night, when she'd been snubbed at the evening tea and had come upstairs feeling more lonely and sad than usual, a sudden thought came to her. She might be the only Christian here where no one seemed to care about religion. But wasn't this a real challenge she needed to take on? Fanny felt a new desire stirring inside her: she would share her faith in Jesus, no matter what the cost! And the cost soon became evident as she determined to live the Christian way. It meant watching her words and deeds and praying now for the girls around her. She could feel the strong enmity whenever she tried to speak about her faith in the Lord Jesus. By the end of her time at the school, there was no big effect that she could see, except that a few of her fellow classmates no longer persecuted her, and some were now affectionate towards her. But there was one very big, unexpected reward, a prize never given before, and Fanny had won it!

The masters of the school had decided that Fanny's papers and her conduct deserved the honorary award called Number One, an honour never before given to any foreigner at Luisenschule! Fanny felt she didn't deserve it, but her joy at hearing the announcement,

'Frances Havergal, Nummer Eins (number one)' kept her from sleep until nearly midnight that night. The whole school assembly had broken out in applause for her, including Olga! Fanny fell asleep still thanking the Lord Jesus.

Her parents' plans were to stay in Germany while her father continued treatment for his eyes. They were proud of Fanny's good work at Luisenschule, but strangely, something else had replaced Fanny's recent joy. Alone in her room that night, she thought she should write in her journal, but what should she write? She had left school forever now! Leaving school was so final and it meant her childhood was over. Now she alone was responsible for any further learning and for her choices for good or bad character. She'd been excused so often as a child, but more would be expected of her now. 'One day I will have to give an account to the Lord for how I've used my mind and heart,' she thought. She remembered so many of her past failures, but almost at once her mind flipped back to a good thing, and then another. Quickly she took up her pen and wrote, 'I will not forget good things to be thankful for. I will be thankful to the Lord for his goodness.' Already a new feeling of joy had started to grow inside, pushing away her fears of what was to come.

Her father and mother were proud of Fanny, their happiness clouded only by the sad fact that once more her father's eyes were not doing any better. His eyesight might be poor, but his good cheer was as great as ever.

'Now, Miss Quicksilver' he said, 'I have decided on a little gift for you, though you will have to stay in Oberkassel with the good pastor Schulze-Berge and his wife and daughter for this gift. Your mother and I will go on to the eye clinic at Heidelberg.'

Fanny threw her arms around him. 'Oberkassel! Oh, Papa, you know I would like nothing better, except for you to see well again.'

'I think, Fanny, you will like staying with the good pastor and his wife and daughter very much indeed. Oberkassel is a pleasant village on the Rhine.' Her father leaned down to whisper in her ear, 'And, you and I know the best scenes will be the mountains nearby.' Fanny's heart beat faster at the thought of mountains. She had loved them since she was a small child. Her father rumpled her hair as he stood straight. 'There is still more. Pastor Schulze-Berge is a fine teacher,' he said, 'and I have arranged for you to enjoy German composition, literature and history under his tutoring.' Her mother smiled in agreement. Fanny's heart sang. She was sixteen, about to be on her own in Germany and studying again! God had known all along how she needed this joy.

From her little room in Pastor Schulze-Berge's house, Fanny could see the Drachenfels Mountains. She could just peek into a narrow rock-shut-in valley, through which the Rhine River flowed from Koblenz. On her desk lay a sketch of her room with its shelves and table covered with German and French books and all she could see through her window, ready to put in her letter to Elizabeth.

'This will not be as good as your sketches, Elizabeth, but it will help you see why I love my room here. Let me tell you how I spend my days. It will soon be dusk, and then I will go down and sit with Pastor Schulze-Berge, a kind and very learned man, who will read aloud, while his pleasant Frau Pastorin and daughter Lottchen, the image of her round-faced smiling mother, work or knit. We talk about what he is reading and it's so helpful. I get up at five, breakfast at seven, then I study for four hours. My books are nearly all in German, and I write papers; I also give one hour to French literature. I do love reading the German poets and Universal History.

'Elizabeth, can you imagine how I enjoy visiting the court of the Count von Lippe, nearby? The dowager countess and the count give half their income away. They are travelling in Italy just now, and I go regularly from 9.00 to 10.00 a.m. to read some German authors with their adopted daughter, Fräulein Von Clondt, whom I like very much and the countess's daughter, Mathilde, who is so gentle though she is often suffering illness. I am invited to tea often and see many of the German aristocracy who visit. One of the countess's daughters is a princess; I do hope she comes to visit while I am there. I have never spoken to a princess!'

'I never hear or speak English now except on Sundays with the English clergy of Düsseldorf. I am even thinking in German! Not many weeks more till I see you — hurrah!'

December came quickly and Fanny was home again in the rectory at St. Nicholas, back in her own small room. Soon life at the rectory was full, visiting in the parish, teaching Sunday school, writing and learning from her father, helping him with music. But something was bothering her more and more. Her confirmation in the Church of England was only months away. Like her friends, she was almost eighteen, the time when they must all decide to take a stand for God and his service before the congregation. They would then take their first communion! No one under that age was allowed to take communion. As the time for her confirmation grew closer, it loomed like a grey cloud instead of the snowy white one in a blue sky that it should have been. Fanny was afraid of one thing. Could she keep this vow to God? If only she felt more love, more sure.

Fanny's confirmation day in the great Cathedral of Worcester had arrived. Built in the Middle Ages and finished in 1564, the Cathedral stood massive inside and out, its vaulted ceilings reaching high above. Fanny walked next to Ellen, a friend, in the procession of those being confirmed, up the great nave beneath towering vaulted arches, found her place near the rail, and sank to her knees. She began to think of who she belonged to – Jesus the Saviour – but stopped as her thoughts flew away, distracted by the chanting of the Litany. Fanny was fourth in line to kneel before the bishop, and her heart beat loudly. The bishop asked her the solemn question each of them must answer:

'Do you renounce sin and all that is opposed to the will of God, hold to faith in God as in the Apostle's

Creed and do you commit yourself to follow Christ as Lord and Saviour?'

Fanny swallowed hard. She suddenly felt alone with God and the bishop. She hardly dared to answer, but then the words came quickly from her heart:

'Lord, I cannot without thee, but oh, with thy almighty help, I do.' When she returned to her seat, tears streamed down her face as she thought she was now more than ever His, even if she did not feel more so. When the bishop gave the closing blessing, it seemed to touch her heart. The bishop, God's minister, was giving them blessings from God! Blessings for her! She would never forget this confirmation day. She would celebrate this day every year all her life!

Fanny was continuing to learn Greek and Hebrew. 'You have a gift for languages, child,' her father said as Fanny read a difficult passage to him. He smiled, closed his Bible and laid aside the large magnifying glass he'd been using to read by. Lately he could not read without the glass at all. Fanny wasn't surprised when her mother announced that her father would try treatment again in Germany. Fanny, whose manuscript book was full of writing she'd already sent to chapter books and magazines, was glad of the time to write. She'd been thinking of a new enigma[1], one she hoped would be fun for readers and accepted by a publisher. It was a little poem that went:

Of a useful whole I'm the most useful part
I've a good circulation, for I've a heart;

---

1. A mysterious puzzle/code.

> *I have two or three garments or outer clothes;*
> *I am closely allied to a lip and nose;*
> *Rags, and parchments, and jewels rare;*
> *Rubbish and treasures within me I bear;*
> *Though I'm often as tall as a spire to view*
> *If you travel far I accompany you;*
> *I am the Indian's light canoe:*
> *And part of a beast of a southern clime;*
> *And finally, now, to crown the whole,*
> *I am your body, but not your soul!*

She needed four more lines to complete this enigma whose answer was a trunk! Many of her poems and enigmas and charades had won prizes, money that she gave to the Church Missionary Society. 'I must show this one to Papa when he returns,' she told herself. Since she'd been a little child, he had stumped the family with his own enigmas and was quite clever at guessing others. He would love helping her with a line or two.

When at last a letter came telling her that not only were they coming home, but her father's eyesight was truly better, Fanny was excited. He would be the one to stand at the reading desk on the coming Sunday for the first time in four years. The family must welcome him home in style.

China roses filled the vines that grew against the rectory, and Fanny gathered them along with greenery enough to fashion a great triumphal arch over the door to Papa's study. At the tip of the arch she attached Papa's crest, also made of flowers. Over the dining room entry, she made a banner with roses to spell out the words,

'Welcome Home.' The family gathered to celebrate his coming home, and Fanny couldn't help but clap for joy at the news he could see! Under the great arch of flowers, all of them knelt with him as he thanked God for all he had done. Fanny thought it was the most beautiful prayer of praise ever, one straight from her father's heart.

The post brought a letter from Elizabeth and that night Fanny wrote back. First she wrote the good news about her father's eyes, and finally came to the things Elizabeth had shared and asked her about.

> *Me too, Elizabeth, I must admit, I do have the same sins and temptations as before. And yes, it's often just as hard work to struggle against them as it used to be, but I take my stand on one thing! Before, I could not see why I should be saved, and now I cannot see why I should not be saved if Jesus died for all ... and on that word I take my stand and rest! ... And I have tasted the sweetness of one new thing, praise! ... One other thing before I close, you recall that my dear sister Ellen and Giles were married in February and live in Ireland? I am to make my first visit to Ireland to stay with them. I can hardly wait ...*

Ellen had written to ask if Fanny would sing for the small group of Irish girls who came weekly to Ellen for Bible study. Fanny had heard about some of the mission work among the Irish people and felt eager to help Ellen bring them the good news of Jesus. She would gladly sing for him.

Mission to Ireland

Cellbridge Lodge, Ellen and Giles' home, was a true Irish country house. A long drive shaded by full green beech trees on each side led to the main house, and Fanny felt as if they were saluting her coming to Ireland. She wanted to learn all she could about this country. The flax and corn mills that Giles owned, the Protestant School where girls came with their headmistress to Ellen's home for a Bible study and of course the Irish Society's work to bring copies of the Bible in Irish for the people to read.

On a visit with Giles to a committee meeting of the Society, Fanny was so moved by the speaker's report that she took a collecting card for the cause. And then the afternoon for Ellen's Bible study came. Fanny tied a small blue ribbon in her hair as Ellen fixed a matching sash about her waist. 'There, you will do fine,' Ellen said. 'The girls are all waiting to hear you sing.' Fanny stood for a moment to whisper a prayer for blessing.

Fanny's voice was clear and true, and the words she spoke between the songs really seemed to reach the young women. They did not want her to stop, and when she finally did their appreciation went straight to Fanny's heart. When one of the girls who heard Fanny sing tried to describe it all to a friend she said, 'Miss Frances, carolling like a bird, flashed into the room like a burst of sunshine and stood before us, her fair, sunny curls falling round her shoulders, her bright eyes dancing and her fresh, sweet voice ringing through the room. I shall never forget that afternoon, never!'

One young Irish girl in Ellen's class longed for what she had seen in Fanny. 'May the Lord teach me, even me, to know and love him so.'

Home again in Worcester, Fanny's Sunday school children were eager to have her back. Fanny kept a record of every child in her class, knew their home life, the important events for each and how they were progressing in class (or not). When young Mark looked as if he had been up all night, she knew there was sickness in the home. She visited them, prayed for them and gladly spent extra time with any student who truly wanted to know more about the Lord Jesus.

Her life at St. Nicholas was full. Fanny wrote and wrote: poems, stories, enigmas, leaflets, chants and soon she was receiving payments to send to the mission's work. Fanny was happy to help with the work in Ireland and this very week was to be the start of a new branch in Worcester for volunteers willing to take collection cards for the Irish work.

The day arrived to open the new branch at a meeting in the Guildhall. After the speaker, an Irish man who gave his own testimony of what hearing the Bible in his own Irish language had done for him, Fanny called for anyone who wanted to join to come to the table in front. A young girl of about twelve was the first to come. Fanny smiled at the earnest look on the child's face. 'Tell me your name,' Fanny said as a sudden idea took hold of her heart, 'because I would like to name our new branch after you, our very first volunteer.' The child blushed and whispered her name. 'What a good name, Bruey,' Fanny said for all to hear, 'and we will now officially be known as *The Bruey Branch*.'

Bruey became one of their best young collectors for the Irish work and dear to Fanny's heart. After young Bruey's sudden death from rheumatic fever, Fanny wrote the story of this little girl whose love for Jesus had touched all those who knew her. The book *Bruey* sold far beyond anyone's imagining and collections poured in. It became one of the best-loved children's books Fanny would write. She received hundreds of letters telling her so, saying the only thing they wished was that young Bruey had not died at the end of the story. But Fanny's answer was always, 'The story is about a real little girl named Bruey who did all those things and her death, though she was so young, was true.'

Maria was going away to their sister Miriam's home at Oakhampton for a visit. 'Fanny, you know it will be good for you if you come with me,' she urged.

Once Fanny would have jumped at the chance to go, but not now. 'Maria, I really can't come. I must stay here and help our mother. Even if I can only run errands it will be helpful.'

Not much later, Fanny became sick. She lay in bed, aching all over, hot with fever and too ill to do anything.

'It's a good thing I didn't go with Maria,' she said as her mother changed the cooling cloth on her forehead. 'I'm so sorry, Mama, for the extra work I am causing.'

'Fanny, you know that nothing comes to us except from the Father's loving hand. You just rest and let others care for you, dear. You will be up and well soon, I'm sure,' her mother said. But it wasn't soon. The fever left but Fanny didn't feel like her old self, and off and on she was stricken with sickness all that summer. On better days she managed to write a little. Today, she was writing to Elizabeth, her dearest friend:

> Yes, my ill health this summer has been very trying to me. I am held back from much that I wanted to do in every way, and have often had to lay poetizing aside … Do you think that these trials can be a kind of powerful medicine Jesus sees that we need … ? I think mine has been a medicine to me lately. You know how easy it always was for me to be merry no matter how things truly were going. But for a time these past months I did feel … forsaken of all cheer, more than I ever felt before. It's given me a real sympathy for others who go through that kind of darkness and longing to be of help, something I lacked before.
>
> I must tell you, Elizabeth, of an incident that will make you laugh, but I hope will bring you the same blessing as it did to me. One day when I was barely out of bed after a wretched week, I truly thought I was going to die! That evening, as I passed the looking glass, I glimpsed myself looking unusually flushed and thought immediately I have

*consumption[1] and will surely die! But I have not one real
sign of being a consumptive. But what if I'd really had the
disease? Would I be ready? Remember the story Jesus told
about the women waiting with their lamps lit for their Lord
to come, five of them ready and five of them foolishly not?
Elizabeth, let's pray that in whatever way or time death
comes to either of us we will be ready for his coming ...*

Autumn brought bright colours to trees. It was a time
Fanny loved. She was well again, though under strict
orders not to overburden her mind. However, no one
was prepared for father's failing health. After so many
years at St. Nicholas, Fanny's father decided to resign.
He could not keep up with the heavy responsibilities of
his large church, and hoped for a smaller, countryside
parish. One in Shareshill, a quiet little parish, was
soon offered to him. It meant that Fanny too would be
leaving behind the cottagers dear to her, and her own
Sunday school class.

Gifts of thanks for her parents long years of service
were showered on them. But it was the small gifts
and words from her Sunday school class that touched
Fanny deeply. 'How shall I ever leave them?' she said
to Maria as they packed. 'They have been in my heart
and prayers so long.'

'I think,' Maria said, 'that they shall not forget
you. And who knows what God has in store for
you next.'

---

1. This is now referred to as Pulmonary Tuberculosis or TB and is an
infection of the lungs.

The rural church of Shareshill, Litchfield was small, but the countryside around it spoke to Fanny's heart of coming spring. They had only been in Shareshill a month when an invitation came by post to Fanny to become a regular contributor to *Good Words* magazine. They had accepted her hymn, *I Gave My Life for Thee*, for publication immediately. Fanny thanked the Lord Jesus. Then, handing her father the letter she had just received, said, 'Papa, I think that writing may be a ministry for me after all.'

Glancing up from the letter, her father smiled. 'Fanny, I expect you will have a ministry with your pen. Just remember that I look forward to being your first reader and critic!' Fanny laughed as she took back the letter. She showed all her writing to her father, sometimes running down the stairs from her room waving a fresh piece in her hand for his approval.

'Papa, what would I do without your help? And not just in my writing. With who else do I get to discuss the Bible, music, books, languages and so much more?'

One day, an invitation came from her brother-in-law Henry and her sister Miriam to come to Oakhampton to tutor her two young nieces; both her father and mother thought the change would be good for her. She would go to Oakhampton.

The New Governess

Fanny could hardly wait to arrive at Oakhampton, the home of her oldest sister Miriam who had married Henry Crane, a well-to-do landowner. Fanny watched from the carriage window as they passed acre after acre, almost 300 rolling acres, stiff with February cold and frozen rose gardens waiting for spring. She remembered how she'd loved visiting Oakhampton as a child. How proud she had been to be an aunt for her two little nieces. How many stories had she written for them and sent when they were only little ones? She loved writing letters to young Constance who had just turned seven, and Evelyn who was eight. She loved the idea of seeing them more and now she would be staying with them! 'O, Lord Jesus, I pray they will like me as their tutor too,' she said softly. And then her fears turned to smiles and laughter. The girls were waiting for her right in front of the great house. Both were bundled in scarves and hats and boots and waving with all their might.

Fanny would have stayed outside to play with the girls if Miriam hadn't ushered her inside. 'I have longed for you to come,' Miriam said, 'and Henry too. I love that you, Fanny, are the one who will give our girls lessons, but outside those short lesson times, you will find our girls will ask you to play all the time, and you will have to be firm about that or they will want to have you all to themselves day and night. We have told them you will kindly be their tutor but you are here as family and this will be your home, Fanny, for as long as you are here.' Miriam hugged her close. 'Oh, Fanny I hope you will enjoy being their tutor.'

Fanny laughed. 'The girls have already written to me about the ponies we must ride, the trips you and Henry have planned at the seashore and abroad, how we will go swimming, skating, play croquet and chess, and if all else fails, they assure me we may do needlework. I don't believe they said a word about lessons, but you know how I love to teach, and it will be even more special teaching my own little nieces.'

Henry, tall and dark-haired like Miriam, had come into the drawing room to welcome Fanny. 'Yes, my dear sister-in-law,' he said, 'Welcome to Oakhampton! And in addition to all of the children's happy plans, I must tell you I have a few of my own. Your talent for writing and singing shall not go unnoticed here.' A serving girl had brought in tea and removed the cover from a plate of warm 'Astley' apple turnovers, Fanny's favourite dessert! As they ate, Henry continued, 'Now, Fanny, if you are interested, I have arranged for you to meet Dr. William Marshall who conducts the Kidderminster Philharmonic Society.' Fanny would soon be singing solos there!

The room Miriam had prepared for Fanny was large and comfortable with a writing table, bookshelves and reading chair, all just the way Miriam knew she would like it. The curtains and drapes were the exact same blue of those their mother had sewn for Fanny's little bedroom at St. Nicholas Rectory! Tears filled Fanny's eyes as she thought of that little room and her own dear mother's last words to her in that house, 'I pray you will be prepared for what God is preparing for you, little one.' Fanny knelt by her new bed and rested her head on the thick coverlet. 'Oh, Lord Jesus, you are preparing me for what you have prepared for me, even now, I know.'

Life was full at Oakhampton, and Fanny's long bout with ill health seemed to be gone as she not only kept up with her energetic, never-still nieces, but outdid them even in ice skating! She had always loved children, and lessons with the girls seemed to fly by. Fanny's own inner drive to keep learning and studying for herself had to be fitted into any small spare time she could find. Fanny got up long before her young charges to start her day with prayer and Bible reading and found she still had time left to go down to the warm kitchen to study.

At lunchtime, while the girls washed before their meal, Fanny, who was far quicker at it, would spend her extra minutes learning Italian verbs. And Fanny could rely on dear old Miss Gundy, the cook, to frown and comment, 'You are studying far too much, Miss Frances.' Fanny smiled, but she kept using her spare moments to study. What she didn't know was that everyone, including Miss Gundy, had been warned that Fanny's health was still the family's concern. Everyone was to take care that she would not over-study and would have time to build up her strength. And it was working! Unbeknown to Fanny, even the weeks of holiday travelling abroad to Germany and meeting her parents in Bonn had all been a part of Miriam and Henry's plan for her while tutoring the girls.

Fanny shared it all with Elizabeth. Ever since school days they had told each other their hopes and fears and joys in their letters. And when Miriam and Henry insisted Fanny take time off to visit Germany, Fanny couldn't wait to share the good news.

Elizabeth, I have such news to tell you! I have finally seen the great Mr. Hiller! You can't imagine how afraid I was to go there. He is the greatest living composer and authority I know, and there I was about to show him my songs! I only hoped to find out if I had talent enough to make music a serious life work for me. He is a quiet little man and received me very kindly. I sat while he read every song and then he said, 'Sincerely and unhesitatingly, I can say that you have.' He has written a few lines to Papa, and believes I should study with a good teacher to gain polish and form in my work. Oh, Elizabeth, it was pleasant to know I have a talent, which I might someday develop, but for now I have no plans to do that. I do want to serve the Lord in any way he plans for me, and more and more I believe that for me to sing for him and witness where I can is what I am to do.

Now for the greatest news of all, something you have been
praying for too: my niece, Evelyn has come to the Lord
Jesus! Her mother Miriam is so happy for her! Keep us
in your prayers, and I you ...

Fanny had just come back from a walk with the girls
and was about to go upstairs when Miriam came from
the parlour holding a letter in her hand. 'Fanny, you
won't guess the good news, Ellen and Giles are moving
to Winterdyne! They will be near us! Ellen says it's such
a beautiful, large country house!' Miriam's face was lit
with excitement. 'You know how Giles was determined
to stay in Ireland during that terrible epidemic of
cholera to help care for his mill workers. Well, at last
the epidemic is over and things are back to normal,
and he feels they can now come to England! Oh, dear,
here, you must read it for yourself.' She handed the
letter to Fanny who began reading it as she headed
back toward the parlour, smiling. The news was so
good that the following week, though Fanny was down
with a feverish cold, she managed to write a poem to
welcome the family home from Ireland.

Alfred and Alice, welcome too!
To an English home and English love
Welcome each little Irish dove;
Never again we hope to be
Kept apart by an angry sea.
A thousand welcomes, O darlings mine,
When we see you at Winterdyne.

More verses followed as Fanny's joy overflowed from the unexpected good news that Ellen and Giles and the children were coming home to England to stay.

Fanny and the girls had decorated the walkway in front of the steps of Oakhampton with garlands of china roses and ivy and signs the children had made to direct everyone to the party, one just for Ellen and Giles and the children. Miriam had ordered a grand feast with plenty of 'Astley' apple turnovers included. Fanny and the girls had put on Sunday dresses for the occasion. 'They will be here any time now,' Fanny said. 'Evelyn, let me fix that pretty blue ribbon of yours in place.'

When Fanny finished the bow, Evelyn, who'd been studying the sparkling emerald ring on her aunt's finger, took hold of Fanny's slender hand to examine it. 'Aunt Fanny, this is such a lovely ring. I should love one just like yours,' she said.

'Evelyn, I would love you to have it, and if you will wait, one day this very ring will be yours to keep,' Fanny said, giving her niece a hug. Neither of them could have known that Evelyn would never own her aunt's ring.

Fanny smoothed Constance's sash and then checked Evelyn's. 'Perfect,' she said, 'at least for now. Knowing you two well, I expect nothing will keep those sashes in place once you run off with your cousins.' She smiled as both girls laughed and ran for the stairs where already there were sounds of the family's arrival. A small stab of sadness touched Fanny's heart as she thought how in just a few months her nieces would be off to school and her days tutoring them at an end. Soon enough the day came and Fanny stood waving and blowing kisses back to them both as the carriage pulled away, taking the girls, ready now at twelve and thirteen, for boarding school.

That evening, as Fanny and Miriam sat near the fire working on frocks for some of the poor children nearby, Fanny said, 'Oh Miriam, I've been wanting to tell you how sorry I am for the burden I've been so often this past year with those old fevers and colds.'

Miriam stopped her work to reply softly, 'Fanny, don't you know how many times your being here has blessed me? The girls could never have blossomed the way they have without you. And I know how you have kept them in prayer, and led them closer to the Lord.' For a moment tears glistened in Miriam's dark eyes. 'Fanny, never have you been a burden here at Oakhampton. And your work for the Lord is an example to us all. And though I know you are planning to make your home with Papa as soon as Mama finds a good retirement home for them, you must think of Oakhampton and Winterdyne as your homes away from home. Ellen and Giles will not have it any other way, nor will Henry.'

Fanny laughed and then became serious. 'No, no, Miriam, but I do love you so. Yet I am laid aside and barely able at times to do even a little. I think the Lord stops me so that I can learn from him what really matters, not just our works, but loving and knowing him.' Fanny smiled and began again to hem the small garment in her hands. 'All the same, I want you to know that I love Oakhampton as well as everyone in it, and will come when I can, if you still want me.'

At that very moment, Henry came striding into the room. 'Want you, Miss Frances Ridley Havergal?' he said, 'not just want you, but we insist on having you here as often as you are able to come.'

And so it was settled. Her parents soon found a new home in Leamington where her father could rest and her mother care for him more easily. Fanny went to stay with them, her heart singing at all the ways she hoped to serve the Lord in Leamington or wherever he led.

Fanny's December birthday was close and she was to take the train for a visit to friends in London. Trains had first come to Worcester when she'd been a girl of thirteen, and to Fanny it was still a treat to travel in one and watch the countryside fly by. She'd also decided to treat herself to a birthday visit to the zoo! In a note to Elizabeth, she wrote all about her trip, ending with, 'You know what a perfect baby I am when it comes to animals.' Elizabeth must have smiled at that, Fanny thought. It was clear to everyone who knew her that she loved animals. The Shaws' young cat, named Brightboots for his white paws, was already the chief character in a children's book she was planning, the story of a cat named, *Ben Brightboots*. She had always loved writing stories for children and this one soon became a favourite.

Fanny no longer had singing lessons with her old teacher Dr. Marshall, but hoped to take a few lessons with Signor Randegger, a well-known teacher and composer in London. 'You have talent, taste, feeling and brains,' the Signor said at their first meeting in his schoolroom, 'but many mechanical difficulties to overcome.' He would have liked her to come to him for a year, but Fanny was satisfied with the few times she could manage. Her first lesson was a lecture on the formation of the throat and production of sound, with homework to write out what she had learned. Instead Fanny put it all into a poem. Fanny waited while her teacher read her work. When he came to her lines about the feminine voice he read aloud:

> But in cavities nasal it never must ring
> Or no one is likely to wish you to sing.

He laughed heartily and Fanny could feel her face turning red; would he think she was making a game of it all? To her relief, he asked for a copy to show his pupils. Her time in London was just enough to fit in three lessons but there would be others.

Back home in Leamington, Fanny was writing, and following her father's wise advice to allow herself to do it slowly. She was also teaching, singing and studying with the small group at the Y.W.C.A.[1] where she was now a member, and it was all going well! She was not prepared for the black bordered letter that came in the post.

---

1. Young Women's Christian Association.

The letter saying that her beloved niece, Evelyn, had died suddenly while at school, lay in her lap while memories of Evelyn's young life flooded over her. For a long time she sat, remembering the happy times. Tears ran down her face, and in her hand lay a small plain gold ring that had been Evelyn's. Miriam had enclosed it as a memorial for Fanny with a little note.

> *Dearest, we remember how our darling Evelyn told us that one day you had promised her that your beautiful emerald ring would be hers. We know how you loved her, and that she would have wanted you to have her ring. Our hearts are broken, but we know we will see our child again …*

It was late, and shadows had darkened Fanny's little room when her tears no longer fell. Gently she picked up Evelyn's small ring and slipped it on her little finger where it would stay. 'Lord Jesus, thank you for this token of love. She is with you now and so happy!' The lovely emerald ring she had promised Evelyn shone as bright as ever, but it was Evelyn's simple ring that she would wear always.

The Mountains of her Dreams

'Fanny dear, you must try to eat all that broth,' Maria insisted. 'Now that your fever is gone, you need to get your strength back.' Fanny smiled and once again sipped the dark beef broth most often given to anyone recovering from severe illness. She had been sick for days but did her best and almost managed to finish it.

Trays of broth, toast and tea were followed with custards and nourishing meals under Maria's care until, at last, Fanny was well enough to be up. A letter from her old classmate and friend, Elizabeth, lay open on her writing table. February's pale sunshine touched the room. It would soon be spring, and a year since young Evelyn had died. Fanny picked up Elizabeth's letter, and suddenly she remembered it was February, Elizabeth's birthday! In a moment her pen was in her hand.

First I send you birthday greetings, Elizabeth, and oh how sorry I was to hear about your accident coming so close to your birthday. As Maria could tell you, I have been wretchedly ill and am not yet quite well enough to enjoy this pause in life. Oh, Elizabeth, remember the Bible verse Isaiah 30:19 that we learned together: 'He will be very gracious unto thee at the voice of thy cry?' It has comforted me so many times. Remember that a cry is like a wordless dart upwards from the heart (not long prayers), and at

*that voice (from our hearts), it's so much more than just a
promise of what he will do; it's what he will be towards us!
What a smile is in those words! My dear brother-in-law
Henry is planning a trip to Switzerland in May with my
sister, Miriam, and their eldest daughter, Miriam Louise,
and, if I am well enough, I am to go too. I shall write and
tell you everything! Do write when you can, and know that
I am praying for you. Love Fanny.*

Fanny couldn't wait to see the Alps, the great snow-
topped mountains. At the age of eight, she'd read about
them, seen pictures of them and she'd longed then
to see them. One she'd heard about was named the
Mountain of Peace. Even her young heart knew then
those unchanging, soaring, snow-capped mountains
would be a place of hushed peace high above the world.
Was she at last about to see what she'd only dreamt
of seeing? The day came and Fanny was finally well
enough to go!

Fanny stepped from the carriage to join Miriam,
her husband Henry and their eldest daughter, Miriam
Louise, at the dock near the boat that would take them
across the English Channel to Calais, France. She could
see the eager look on her young niece's face. Miriam
Louise's dark hair and eyes were the image of her
mother's. As Fanny hugged her she said, 'Could this
young lady possibly be my niece, the one I used to send
my childish stories to?'

'Oh, Aunt Fanny, I still have those stories. Who else
has an aunt that wrote stories when she was only eight

years old for her toddler niece?' Her hug left Fanny nearly breathless. 'I'm so glad you are coming with us. We'll have such fun together.'

Fanny's sister, Miriam, hugged her too. 'This trip will be good for us all,' she said. 'I think it will help heal our hearts, dear.' Fanny knew that Miriam still mourned the loss of her little Evelyn.

Fanny wiped away a tear that threatened to fall and turned to Henry. 'Ah, a man ready to guide and guard his charges, if ever I saw one.' She laughed as Henry, tall and strongly built, swept her up into a welcoming hug.

As they boarded the boat, the skies began to turn grey with heavy clouds. The channel waters could churn and behave badly in sudden storms, and Fanny was prepared.

First she chose a spot in the lee of the deck cabin where her sister and niece rested. This was a good spot on the ship as it was the most sheltered from the wind. It was no use going below with the others as she knew she would be sick. Fanny's shawl did for a mattress, her carpet bag for a pillow, a pile of tarpaulin for a back rest, and with a cape of waterproof over her head and pinned under her chin, she was ready. She lay down and pulled a tarpaulin to cover her, all but her nose.

Miriam Louise had come up to see how her father and aunt were doing. 'You will be walked over, Aunt Fanny,' she said. 'You don't look like a human being!' Fanny giggled. Her brother-in-law didn't look like one either. He was cased in a tarpaulin coat down to his heels, with a hood which stuck up in two stiff points, leaving little of his face visible besides his beard.

For the first half hour, she and Henry joked, then slept a bit, then asked after each other and then silence as the crossing became truly rough. Poor Miriam was soon heartily seasick.

By the time they arrived at Brussels that evening, Fanny was amazed that her sister, who had seemed so poorly and 'about to die', was ready to go sightseeing. The three Cranes went off, but Fanny, who only a month ago had been ill, stayed at the hotel to rest, and soon would be so glad that she did.

A little while later, one of the Belgian maids wearing a white, frilled cap tied under her chin came to the room, and, seeing Fanny on the sofa, asked, 'Oh, Miss, are you not well?'

'No, no, it's just the long trip from England that has tired me,' Fanny explained, 'especially the rough crossing we had over the English Channel.'

The maid shook her head. 'I have never understood how it is that England is all surrounded by water.'

'Come, sit down and let me try to explain it to you,' Fanny offered. Soon the two were talking of other things, and Fanny learned that the girl had been near death last year when a fearful illness raged through Brussels. Soon Fanny was telling her of the one who heals our diseases. The maid shuddered as she told Fanny how terrible it was to think that one must die, and all alone.

For half an hour they talked, and when she left, she promised Fanny she would come back in the morning. Fanny would be ready!

When the maid, whose name was Victorine, did come the next morning, Fanny handed her a French St. John's Gospel, one of many she had brought along hoping to give them out wherever she could. 'This is for you, Victorine. I have marked the good things I think you will be glad to read, all of them pointing to Jesus for peace, the promise of eternal life and salvation.' Victorine promised to read it and left thanking her. Fanny's heart was light. She would pray for Victorine. It had been so wonderful to speak to this young woman about Jesus in her own French language! Fanny was so grateful for God's gift to her for learning languages. She was at home in French as in English or German as well as in several other languages. That night, Fanny wrote her first journal entry about the trip, including her visit with Victorine!

At breakfast, Henry explained their travel plans to Switzerland by way of the Rhine route to Heidelberg, Freiburg, Basle and Schaffhausen. Fanny informed him she planned to keep journal notes of each place they visited. Scenes from the Rhine were so lovely that she wrote about them with joy. On the last day of their boat trip on the Rhine, Fanny met an elderly gentleman who spoke English with a strong, strange accent. He was travelling with his daughter, a shy girl with a gentle, sad expression, whose sweet smile seemed to light her face. Fanny wondered if they were Jews, and later in the day she asked the young girl. The girl's face coloured deeply as she said, 'Yes.'

Quickly Fanny said, 'How I wish that I too were of Jewish blood!' Astonishment filled both the girl's face and her father's.

'You stand alone,' he said, his voice bitter. 'Other Christians feel very differently toward us.' Fanny spoke, then in German and the two had a long talk. 'Yes,' he said, 'I honour Jesus of Nazareth: He was a wonderful man. But as for his being God ...' He didn't finish the sentence, and for some time they talked as Fanny explained how Jesus's claim to be God must either be true, or else Jesus was an impostor and a liar. Finally, Fanny turned to his daughter, who had been listening, and spoke to her about the love and tenderness and sympathy, everything we need that is in Jesus. That night, in her journal, Fanny wrote her simple plan for telling anyone she could about Jesus: 'Tell them what you know is true. Tell them what he is to you!'

In Schaffhausen, Fanny and Miriam Louise walked by their first Swiss lake! The next stage of their journey by rail took them past sharply peaked mountains unlike any they had yet seen. At last in Berne, Switzerland, they reached the Berner Hof and from the windows in their rooms they would be able to see the Alps as the mist that hid them lifted.

Fanny was asleep, but she woke as Miriam Louise quietly crept past to the window. 'Anything to see?' she called.

'Oh yes, I really do see them,' Miriam Louise said in an awed voice. Fanny rushed from her bed. The sun had risen above the thick mist, and to the southeast were giant outlines bending towards the sun. Majestic mountains so great they far out-topped the green hills below them. That morning, they took the train to Thun and soon saw the Alps along the way. In the afternoon, Henry took them all for a two-hour sail on the lake, and there above them Fanny saw close up for the first time the Jungfrau, the Monch and the Eiger, so still and mighty.

Fanny could only whisper, 'So now the dream of all my life is realised, and I have seen snow mountains! They are just as pure and bright and peaceful as I dreamt them.' In Lauterbrunnen, they stayed at the foot of the Jungfrau and that day climbed to the most breathtaking view of the Alps that Fanny could have imagined.

The path upward was a series of sharp, steep zigzags and shelves over precipices. At one place, when they dismounted their sure-footed horses to look down at the valley 925 feet (282 metres) below, their guide became anxious. 'You must hold fast by the small trees,' he said, 'A slip on that mossy bank would be too awful to think of.' When at last they came out above the forest, the Jungfrau was directly opposite them, the centre of a magnificent view of towering Alps, all of them giants with perpendicular sides, glaciers, avalanche tracks, snow-fields, everything Alpine! Even the grasses at their feet were sheets of flowers all around them, tiny and exquisite. Fanny's favourites were the blue Alpine forget-me-nots. She knew she would never forget this sight of God's handiwork, so powerful and marvellous wherever one looked. The whiteness of the snow on the mountains was purer than she could have imagined, and at once she thought of the Bible's words, 'whiter than snow.'[1]

Fanny would also never forget an incident of sheer terror and delight that happened further along on their trip. It was a hot July day, and Henry decided to boat across the lake at Vevey. Miriam and Fanny's niece stayed behind to rest while Fanny and Henry explored. The area was not one in the guidebooks, but so beautiful they decided to climb to the nearest Swiss village on the mountain above them. The little village at the boat dock had only one donkey and one horse to lend them, but both were being used somewhere, and the owners assured them that with patience and perseverance they could climb up the gorge to the little village of Novelles. After two and a half hours of steep climbing in the heat, they were exhausted and hungry. They found a small inn that looked to Fanny much like a hen roost.

Inside, the tiny kitchen was dark with a pot hanging over a fire of sticks on a large hearthstone. The innkeeper was overjoyed to invite them in and seated them at one of the three small tables and benches. For lunch they were served a loaf of fresh black bread and a plate with three funny little cheeses and the usual Swiss

---

1. Psalm 51:7.

wine. He offered an egg, and while it boiled, he sent round the village hoping to get some butter which was only made half an hour higher up the mountain. After lunch, Fanny asked him if he had a horse they might use to go down, but his horse was gone to pasture. 'Trust me, Mademoiselle,' he said. 'I will arrange something for you.'

'We are not particular,' Fanny said, 'a hay cart would do.' He smiled and hurried out.

When he returned a while later, dressed in a white shirt, he said, 'The horse is ready!' Fanny could barely believe her eyes as she followed Henry outside. A hay sledge with two small wheels behind and two thick runners lay on the ground. An old wine chest with a plank across it was tied onto the sledge as a seat. Two long, crooked sticks were tied to the runners for shafts. Carefully, Fanny climbed in next to Henry. 'Now, Monsieur, we will go like the wind,' their host cried; picking up the shafts, he was off running like a mad man, tearing downhill. In spite of Fanny's cries to be careful, he only glanced round laughing as he leapt over boulders and holes, swung round corners on the very edge of the deep gully, till she would have been badly frightened if she and Henry were not laughing so hard. Their 'horse' stopped once to get his breath and talk about how he would patent his invention for the next fair and make his fortune!

They were a quarter of a mile from the bottom when suddenly the sledge swung round a corner, swerved into fallen rocks and sent them all flying! Fanny and Henry were bruised and shaken, but not seriously hurt, and glad to find their host the same. While Fanny brushed off dirt and splinters, Henry paid the little man for the sledge that lay in pieces around them. They said goodbye and their host, as jolly as ever, called out to them, 'Be sure to tell everyone at the hotel what a first-rate carriage I will have ready for them next time, if they will come to our little village inn!' Fanny and Henry turned away again and burst into laughter. That night, Fanny chuckled as she wrote it all down in her journal.

When the trip was over, the journal would speak to her again and again of the wonders she'd seen and felt here.

The day for the last entry had finally come. They were leaving Switzerland! As their train took them away from Neuchatel, Fanny and Miriam Louise strained to see their last glimpse of the Alps. When Fanny could no longer see any trace of the giant mountains, she settled back beside Miriam Louise. 'Do you think we shall ever see them again?' she asked. 'We've seen such wonders of God's creation, it makes me think of the Bible verse: "The works of the Lord are great, sought out of all them that have pleasure therein."'

'Oh, I already want to come back again, and we're not even home!' her niece said.

---

2. Psalm 111:2.

The Queen is Pleased

'Fanny, you have only just come home and are you off again so soon? You scarcely have had time to rest, child,' her mother said, looking up from the lace collar she was stitching. 'I only wonder about your health, my dear.' Her mother's look of displeasure seemed clear to Fanny. But before Fanny could say a word, her father interrupted.

'Now, now, my dear, I suspect that our Fanny, though she is truly a young lady of thirty-two, is still my little Quicksilver grown-up, and looking quite well these days. And I suppose you are only too glad, child,' he said to Fanny, 'to be off to London?'

'Oh, yes, Papa, I am excited to go to London. And I am hoping too that the trip to visit dear friends in Scotland afterwards will be as good for me as this summer's trip to Switzerland has been.'

Her father smiled broadly. 'Yes, you will love the Scottish highlands just as you loved all of God's outdoors as soon as you could toddle. And having your first book of poems, with its fine title, *The Ministry of Songs*, published in London is no small reason for a visit to London, either.' Her father chuckled and her mother joined him, and Fanny did too before she hugged them both. Her father understood her well. He knew how she loved God's creation, how it spoke to her heart because it spoke to his too. And he knew especially how music and songs did the same. He had served the Lord he loved all his life with his music, as she now longed to do.

London was warm in August as Fanny visited first her publisher and next her singing teacher, Signor Randegger. After her very first lesson with him when she had written a poem in a homework assignment, and the Signor had read it to all his students, he'd asked her to bring him more! He was delighted to see her, and had an offer to make her, which he hoped she would not refuse. They talked for several minutes. 'So you see, my dear,' he said, 'if you will write the songs, and allow me to set them to music, I believe we may offer a new song book especially for children.'

Fanny would have hugged the great man, if her respect for him had not at once taken the upper hand. 'I can barely imagine your wonderful music together with any of my songs, and yet I think that your music will surely transform them.'

'Then it is settled and we shall see this work through!' Signor Randegger said. 'I should like twelve songs by the end of October, if you will agree.'

Fanny didn't stop to think as her words tumbled out, 'Yes, oh yes, I do truly agree with all my heart!'

Her visit with friends in Scotland to see the Scottish Highlands only made her heart sing even more. In September she visited Winterdyne, and while there she wrote a fourteen-stanza poem about a shipwreck during a terrible storm. The things she'd seen and heard on her visit to Scotland were still fresh in her mind. The story told of a daring rescue, where the sailors on board the doomed ship must hold fast to the rope thrown to them, but let go of the mast at the trumpet-signal, 'Now!,' if they were to survive. Only one man who could not dare to let go of the mast drowned with the sinking ship. Fanny wrote in the last stanza:

> *God's 'Now' is sounding in your ears;*
> *Oh, let it reach your heart!*
> *Not only from your sinfulness*
> *He bids you part;*
> *Your righteousness as filthy rags*
> *Must all relinquished be,*
> *And only Jesus' precious death*
> *Must be your plea.*
> *Now trust the one provided rope,*
> *Now quit the broken mast,*
> *Before the hope of safety be*
> *Forever past.*
> *Fear not to trust his simple word,*
> *So sweet, so tried, so true,*
> *And you are safe for evermore;*
> *Yes, even you!*

Fanny put down her pen that night, thinking, 'I did not plan to write this, Lord, it simply came. There are so many shipwrecked who need to hear the message of you, their only hope. Oh help me bring your "Now" to them.'

Back at home in Leamington, poems came spilling out. They just couldn't wait to be written. Fanny had a ready critic at hand in her father who patiently listened to all her new works. But life wasn't completely taken up with writing. When she wasn't busy putting pen to paper, she was teaching Bible study or Sunday school class, writing letters, working for the Church Missions, the Irish Society which she loved, keeping commitments to her Y.W.C.A. sisters, or visiting the poor. One of her September visits to a cottage family, with a young baby, inspired her to write *Baby's Turn* on feeding sweet fruit to a baby and dreaming of the grown woman this child would be one day.

It was the 18th of October before Fanny worked in earnest on the songs for Signor Randegger. By the 24th of October all twelve were finished. They were to be called *Sacred Songs for Little Singers* and published by the London Publisher to the Queen. Fanny had prayerfully dedicated the book to the Queen's youngest daughter, Beatrice. Her father, Prince Albert, had died when Beatrice was only four years old. The princess was now thirteen, and still her mother, Queen Victoria, mourned the loss of Beatrice's father. The Queen still dressed in black mourning clothes and was seldom in public. Fanny's heart went out to the little princess.

The dedication page read: 'Dedicated, by the gracious permission of Her Majesty, to Her Royal Highness the Princess Beatrice.' In the third song, titled *Evening Prayer*, Fanny had written as the last stanza:

> *Thou my best and kindest Friend;*
> *Thou wilt love me to the end!*
> *Let me love Thee more and more,*
> *Always better than before.*

This was the truth she longed for the little princess, and all children to know; Jesus was the friend they needed. She loved children, the difficult ones of her Sunday school classes, those easy to love, the children of the poor she visited, her own nieces and nephews to whom she could never write enough and the children she only heard about through the missions that reached out to them in other countries and here in England. And she loved writing for them stories, poems, songs, Bible study lessons, letters, and was quick to answer every child's letter to her.

Fanny was warmly welcomed home by her father. 'You look happy,' he said, 'and your Mama will be glad to see how well too, as soon as she brings us those 'Astley' apple turnovers she makes so well. Don't tell her that I know she made them just for you.'

'Papa, you know Mama spoils you terribly, and thanks to her loving care, you do look so much better these days. I have so much to tell you both.' Between tea and apple turnovers, Fanny told them of her adventures big and small. After that, there was the stack of mail waiting for her to see, and Fanny was soon at her desk.

One of her children's books, *Ben BrightBoots*, was published in 1869 and was selling well, according to a letter from her publisher. She smiled, remembering the children's kitten at Winterdyne, the cat that had given her the idea for *Ben BrightBoots*. Her stories for children, like *Bruey* and *Arthur Phillips* and *The Four Happy Days,* were all based on true stories that she felt needed to be written down for children. 'Whatever gift of writing, however small, Lord,' she whispered, 'may it ever only be for your use.' Fanny smiled again; she loved imagining every story, and that was another gift from God, to so enjoy the work he gave her. The cheques she received for her work were a joy too as she gave all she could to help with missions.

A letter from a friend, Julia, reminded Fanny of how thankful she was too for the power of music and its ministry. Fanny thought Julia's writings were among the best she knew. Julia had been very ill, and had sent her a poem about her longing to hear Fanny sing the gospel songs, like *Abide with me*, or *Nearer My God to Thee*, songs she knew would comfort her. Julia's poem began:

> *Ask her to come and sing to me,*
> *For day by day I long,*
> *With a craving never known before,*
> *For the magic of a song —*
> *'T were like a sweet, stray wanderer*
> *From heaven's choral throng.*

The last two lines of the poem read:

> *I know she'll come and sing for me*
> *Some old familiar strain.*

Fanny wrote back:

> *Dearest Julia,*
> *How I do wish I had known! It would have been the most*
> *exquisite pleasure to have come to sing to you. I know that*
> *longing for music so well, though I do not think many know*
> *what it is. Sometimes I have thought that this very 'music-*
> *thirst' ... is from God ... to lead us ... to that which stills*
> *all longings, the music of his name.*

Fanny paused in her letter thinking about how many times
she had found music truly reaching hearts in a way words
alone didn't. She thought back to the time in Ireland where
she'd sung for the Irish girls in Ellen's Bible study, and then
of another time at a gathering for musicians and singers.
Both had brought someone to seek the Lord. She picked
up her pen to finish her letter to Julia:

> *Julia,*
> *I know that music for me is a way to serve the Lord Jesus.*
> *Once I was offered the part of the wicked Queen Jezebel*
> *in a cantata, but thanks to wise advice I did not take the*
> *part. I could not sing the part with all my heart, and you,*
> *dear one, will understand how I wanted to sing with all my*
> *heart songs that would turn others to Jesus. I thank him for*
> *you, and the gifts he has given you to serve him.*
> *Yours,*
> *F.R.H.*

It was not long after this that young Julia died and
in her sadness at the news, Fanny knew that at last

her dear friend was truly hearing the music of His name.

Life at Leamington was busy as Fanny continued to write and to sing whenever she was asked and could. This morning she had heard her father playing one of his songs. He had been making music all his life. She would never earn medals for her music the way he had, or, like him, write a hymn so beautiful that it was sung in churches all over England, but thanks to him she knew how to sing and compose and play piano. She couldn't remember a time when the Havergal family gatherings didn't ring with his strong voice leading them all in song. A sigh escaped Fanny's lips. Her father was not as strong these days as she would like. One day sorrow would come to this house at Leamington, and she wondered would it be her father or herself on whom it fell?

A Sudden Sorrow

'Here,' Fanny said, 'let me take the tray for you, Mama. Mmm, it looks and smells good. Papa will love these warm pancakes you've made for him.' They were headed to the sitting room where Papa was playing one of his songs. 'Your loving care of Papa has helped him so much, Mama. He looked so well at morning prayers today.'

'Your father's health does seem to be improving, child,' her mother said. 'Your being here with us helps, too, my dear. He enjoys working with you on your poems and songs. I believe it does him good. Only remember you must not overtax him or your own strength either!' Fanny nodded as they entered the sitting room. Her mother was always careful to remind her of what she called Fanny's 'frail health', and though Fanny knew she truly cared, it sometimes vexed her to hear it so often. And that was sure to be followed by feelings of guilt over being irritated about such a thing. It felt especially bad when friends and family saw only her outer cheerful nature, and would not have dreamt that she failed to be the same inside.

In letters to Elizabeth, she was free to talk about how she failed so often as a Christian. 'Oh sometimes,

The Girl who Loved Mountains

Elizabeth, it seems when I look back, my life has been a series of crags, rugged places to climb and deep valleys to cross with so many shadows,' she wrote. 'Pray for me, as I pray for you …'

'Now Papa, please try to just sing as we play this beautiful song of yours.' There was nothing like listening to her father play when he made melodies as he went along, but she loved hearing him sing as he used to do. Now she often had to coax him to try to sing even when she played one of his hymns. His greying hair still curled, and she thought of him still as her handsome, godly father, so full of wisdom, and her best teacher and critic! As they finished a round of songs, it was clear that he looked ready to stop. 'Papa, that was wonderful! I think I need to run upstairs to my desk for a while and finish that new poem I want you to look at for me. Besides, I think we both need a little rest before we tackle one or two hard questions I have about the new poem.'

'Off with you then, my little Quicksilver. I will certainly need my rest if I am to be your teacher,' he teased.

Fanny's feet did fly up the stairs to her room where a great pile of work waited for her, including the poem she wanted to show her father. His sight was failing but his gifted ear for music and his fine mind were as sharp as ever, letting nothing slip by unnoticed. At her desk, she picked up her pen to write, but her eyes strayed first to the window next to it. It was almost April and early spring had begun. As always, the seasons, the clouds, the things of nature spoke to the deepest parts of her, telling of God's hand in them. Was it from her father she had first learnt to feel that blessing? She thought for a moment of Astley, her childhood home at the church rectory, its fields and little stream and all the trees father had planted there, trees of every kind. How he loved them, and she had learned to love them too. Tears filled her eyes; he had asked to be buried by a certain great fir tree, one of his favourites in the Astley church cemetery. How would she bear not hearing his voice explaining something from the Bible he loved so? Or not listening to his gifted fingers playing music he had written, songs lifting her heart to heaven? And who would she go to with her questions? Only recently, she had visited a church and come away shaking her head because it had been all pleasant stories about the Bible, but very little about what God's Word was saying; certainly not how her father would have taught it! Smiling, she dried her eyes, and came back to the work in front of her. As her father would say, 'All things work together for good to those who love him, so let's praise him, shall we?' 'Yes, yes, Papa, that is just what we must do,' she whispered.

Easter came and the family gathered for celebration. Fanny and Miriam both noted how unusually well their father was as they took a walk with him. 'You must let me play and sing for you this afternoon, my dears,' he said. 'I have composed a tune just this morning

that I believe you will like.' It was his last song on
earth. On Easter Day he fell asleep and did not regain
consciousness. He was buried at Astley under the great
green fir that he loved, and Fanny felt as if her heart
would truly break.

In a letter to Elizabeth, a few weeks later, Fanny
wrote:

> *You know how sad I have been. Last night, I heard one of
> Papa's chants gloriously sung at the Westminster Abbey
> evening service, verses from Exodus 3:7: 'I have surely seen
> the affliction of my people which are in Egypt, and have
> heard their cry by reason of their taskmasters, for I know
> their sorrows.' It struck me that there is sorrow that shows
> clearly and sorrow that is hidden like the secret one ... you
> can only tell a friend, and there is sorrow so deep inside us
> sometimes that no eye can see it, no ear hear it, only God's.
> It was so comforting to me that he sees and hears our deepest
> cry and knows our sorrows whatever kind they are! ...*

Fanny felt the loss of her father deeply as she worked on
his collection of hymns for the publication of the *Havergal's
Psalmody*. As she began to read one hymn in particular her
eyes filled with tears: 'Thou art the helper of the fatherless.'
This was meant for her. 'Thank you, Lord, for this special
promise to your orphans,' she whispered. She was an
orphan now, and God would help her even with the music.
And he did. Fanny wrote several new songs for *Songs of Grace
and Glory* which was doing well, and this time an old friend
who looked at them had only praise for them! She was in
the habit now of asking God's help each time she wrote.

Her father was gone, and without him Fanny's stepmother began to centre her attention and time on Fanny and the work she was doing. Fanny was determined that, God helping her, she would do her wishes in anything, at any cost, but it was becoming more and more difficult.

The new *Havergal's Psalmody* was about ready and the conflict between Fanny and her mother over it was growing. One morning, as Fanny finished writing her name on the page before her as the editor and showed it to her mother, her mother frowned. 'Now, Fanny,' she said, 'I do wonder if you really ought to put your name here as editor. It seems so distracting, don't you think?' She also thought all of Fanny's own tunes in the collection should simply be initialled F.R.H.

'I hadn't thought about that at all,' Fanny said. She did not say that she felt the opposite about being recognised as the editor. 'But I do agree with you, Mama, that my initials on my tunes will be less conspicuous, and I do not want them to stand out. Everyone will think how bold I was to have written them at all.'

'Yes,' her mother said, 'I quite agree with you. It certainly would be wise just to use your initials on your tunes. We really must be most careful about this Psalmody and I am sure it will be well received. Your father was such a great musician.' Her mother turned to go and Fanny put the page she had been working on aside.

Her full name as the editor would have been an introduction to the public and given her an advantage she would not have again to be so recognised in the field of music. She had worked hard for months editing the music, composing, and had earned the right to be recognised as the editor. It would help her whole future path. But her mother's wishes were clear: that Fanny would not put her name on the book as editor, but let the *Havergal's Psalmody* be anonymously edited. Fanny sighed deeply. For her, something greater was at stake. She could feel the vexation growing like a weed inside her. 'Oh, Papa, how I miss you,' she whispered. If it wasn't for friends like Pastor Blake and his wife, who had helped her through these months since her father's death, whatever would she have done? 'That's it, the Blakes! I know they want to help and I can rely on their prayers.' Quickly she took up her pen and wrote to them, asking them to pray that she would do the right thing.

In her letter she wrote,

My mother has given me too many plain hints for me to pretend not to know her wishes in this matter, and I have definitely set before myself, God helping me, to do her wishes. But this is a sacrifice for me, and I cannot say I have made it cheerfully. I only do it because it is the right thing to do and I really want to please my mother. Will you pray that I may have grace not to do it regretfully and reluctantly, but to feel rightly and be right in God's sight? I want to really live the Christian life to please him. Your kindness and loving help since Papa's death have meant so much to me, and I do need your prayers in this.

The *Havergal's Psalmody* was published with an anonymous editor, and Fanny wrote to the Blakes to tell them. 'Thank you, thank you! Your prayers have been answered. The deed is done, and Mama is pleased that I have not put my name on the new *Havergal's Psalmody*. And on Sunday morning, I felt so moved to give myself to Jesus, that I asked him to make me more entirely His than ever before, every gift, every part of me to serve him. It has all turned out for my good, my vexation is gone, and I have peace. I cannot thank you both enough for your praying about this. Just see what a joyous turn-about he has brought!'

Soon it would be Fanny's birthday and already letters from friends had come and waited to be answered. Only one envelope among the pile was banded with the black sign of mourning, and Fanny opened it. As she read, tears spilled down her face. Her friends, the Snepps, had just lost their baby. Fanny, who had known such grief this year, knew she needed to write at once.

Dear, dear Mrs. Snepp,
What can one do but just weep with you! I can only guess what this sorrow is. . . . That dear little beautiful thing! He looked so sweet and happy when I saw him at the station . . . Oh, if only you could see him now, how beautiful he must be now that he has seen Jesus and shines in the light of God . . . I know we can't comfort, only Jesus can; and I shall go and plead long and intensely for this as soon as I have closed my letter . . . He knows what human love is and he must be specially touched in such a sorrow . . .
Yours with deepest sympathy and love.

To one friend, who was worn out with sorrow and illness, Fanny advised, 'Do not pray any more, or you will be the worse for it. I hope you will not do anything unnecessary while you are away. We have committed this to God; he has heard, and he knows … you … need rest. Our bodies are only clay, not iron and brass. Do not even write a word to me that isn't necessary until your eyes and head are better ….'

As Fanny thought about her own struggles with illnesses, she knew how they had taken away the energy to write or sing, time and time again or do any work steadily ever since her twenties. Her words of comfort and advice to others came because she could truly encourage others with the comfort God had given her.

Christmas was close now and Fanny had more invitations to sing than ever. Tonight she was to sing sacred music and her father's Christmas carols at Mr. Bromley's annual parochial tea party for 500 poor people. Fanny hugged her mother as she said, 'How grand and how bright it will be, and I am so happy. And on Wednesday, Mama, I am to give an evening's sacred music to the patients in the Hydropathic here.' The building was quite near Leamington and many sick went there to take the waters, hoping for a cure.

'You must be careful, child, not to overtax yourself,' her anxious mother said. 'There is always so much to do at this season, and I do appreciate your help, dear.'

'And I love helping you,' Fanny said. She really did try to help with errands and whatever her mother needed doing, though her own schedule was especially busy these days. Fanny smiled, remembering a recent large party where she had sang, praying the songs she chose would bring a clear message. Later, the pastor who was there had thanked Fanny for her sermon in song! When she left, her own heart was singing. This was what her singing, and her writing, any gift God gave her was meant for: to serve him!

More and more she was invited to sing at gatherings in large households, and always someone wanted to talk with her in private. Fanny left each time with new burdens, sometimes sad secrets and heavy spiritual problems that people who needed help shared with her. Her brother-in law, Henry, liked to tease her that everyone was making plans to talk to her alone from visitors right down to the servants. 'Henry wouldn't have teased me,' she thought, 'if he knew how exhausted I feel after such times.' Sometimes she almost dreaded an invitation to a large household. But she could not give up ministering to young women who often felt so overwhelmed by their lives. If only she could influence them wisely and earnestly. 'Please pray for me that I will do well in ministering to young women,' she wrote to Elizabeth, and those in her Y.W.C.A. group.

In June, Fanny visited the Snepps and together with Mr. Snepp worked on the hymnal *Songs of Grace and Glory*. Fanny's father had written the last of his own hymns for it just before his death. The hymnal was considered to be the most comprehensive in the

Church of England. There were hymns and tunes for every season, every belief of the church, every part of the Christian life and all of them needed to be arranged, sometimes restored, and sometimes even their author's names and dates needed finding. Fanny and Mr. Snepp had many answers to prayer as they puzzled often where to look and what to select. Fanny loved the work and even wrote some hymns and tunes for the collection while she was there. When it was time to return home to Leamington, Fanny left thinking how her father would have loved to be part of all this, and yet it was because he had taught her all she knew about music she'd been able to do it!

Fanny's mother had a list of visits they needed to accomplish when she got back and a list of other things she thought Fanny might help her with. Fanny also had her own invitations, editor's requests, letters of thanks, requests for advice. The letters from her growing family of nieces and nephews were especially loved. Fanny put her arm about her mother's shoulder. 'Now, what do you think we ought to do first, Mama?' Her mother looked pleased, and it felt good to Fanny to see her smile.

In the Alps Again!

In her letter to Elizabeth, Fanny wrote,

Oh, Elizabeth, are we really going? I am so excited about all the things you suggested. Just think, we will soon be climbing mountains, seeing God's marvels, finding little Swiss inns all on our own! Our copy of The Practical Swiss Guide *ought to be enough for us to find out what we need. Are you are longing to be off, the way I am, simply going at our own pace and choosing what we think best to do. I did have to promise Henry and Miriam, and almost everyone, that I will take no dangerous risks. Thankfully we will have only our carpet bags and knapsacks to carry about with us. I have already stuffed my carpet bag with French Gospel tracts and small books to give away, and I know you are bringing as many as you can too, the rest can be sent on ahead of us. Let's pray that we may be ready to tell of Jesus' love anywhere, any time we can.*

Dear Henry has promised to see us off. He is quite certain that we will find the first part of the trip into France more difficult, even though the war between France and Prussia is over. The French people have suffered so much, and we are bound to see some of the devastation of war on our way through to Switzerland. Since we are not travelling the usual tourist routes, it may be harder to find the kind of lodging we want (cheaper), but Henry is sure we will find the trains safe and running. The whole family will be expecting to hear from us along the way, and both our guide book and the locals will tell us where posting and receiving letters is best. My plan is to write circular letters[1] instead of to individuals, and Henry has promised to see that each letter is circulated to everyone on my list. Have you managed to find all the things we agreed to bring? I wish we didn't need to carry those bulky waterproofs, but I expect we will need them. I am so glad we will be wearing plain, good quality travelling clothes and each of us has sturdy boots, and I plan to get some Swiss fellow to put those heavy nails into the soles of mine for our mountain climbing, and you might want to do that too. Elizabeth, can you believe that in only days we shall not be writing to each other, but talking face to face? I can hardly wait! Pray for me as I for you …

The plan was to go by way of the French route to Basle, Switzerland by train. In Paris there was time to walk about, but at once Fanny felt the difference between the old, colourful, happy atmosphere of the Paris she'd seen before and what she saw now. Elizabeth felt it too. 'Look, Fanny,' she said, 'how many of the women are wearing black signs of mourning. I have heard there were many husbands and sons lost in the war with Prussia.'

Fanny nodded. 'Yes, there is so little colour, no grand flower stalls; the whole city is in mourning,' she said. 'Maybe a few of the market women would take some tracts.' Each of them went in opposite directions and soon had given out many French tracts, and those who took them seemed grateful to get them. It was

---

1. Letters sent to a large group of people at the same time.

time to get the train to Belfort where they hoped to see some of the historic sights and find lodging for the night.

At Belfort there were scenes of wrecked houses, roofless and some only open floors like a doll's house, others in total collapse, and heaps of devastating ruins were everywhere. Almost right away Fanny and Elizabeth found themselves giving away many of their stock of little French books and tracts. At one place, a tall, unsmiling man who looked official to Fanny, seemed to be watching them, and when he approached, Fanny thought he meant to tell them to stop. Instead, he politely asked Elizabeth, 'Would it be possible for me to have one of those, and if you can spare two, I would be grateful?' Elizabeth was quick to give him two, and he thanked her as if she had given him some great thing. They found one place where wounded soldiers seemed hungry to receive the tracts, and Fanny's eyes filled with tears as they left with calls of 'merci' all around them. Their supply of little books was nearly gone. Fanny wished they'd had hundreds more with them.

Travelling by train from Belfort to Basle and straight through to Lucerne at times took them high above deep ravines and across freshly built bridges that seemed less than sturdy. It was when they were on the train to Lucerne and the evening sky was beautifully clear that Fanny cried out, 'Oh look, Elizabeth!' and pointed to a distant range of snow mountains, their first sight of the Alps! The setting sun lit the snow-topped mountains perfectly golden. It lasted for almost five minutes, and Fanny could only say, 'It's like a vision of the gate to the heavenly city in John Bunyan's *Pilgrim's Progress*. Nothing I have ever seen on earth is like it, for me.' Turning to look at Elizabeth, Fanny saw tears pooling in Elizabeth's dark eyes. This was Elizabeth's first time to see such a sight, and it had touched her heart too. She understood just what Fanny meant.

They were in Switzerland and free of any need to hurry, free of all the demands they'd left behind at home, and even the Swiss air felt refreshingly good! With nothing to stop them, they began enjoying the sights, the climbs, all the things they chose to see and do together.

In one of her first letters home, Fanny wrote:

This morning we walked seven miles to Wasen, not hurrying. But then how could we hurry! There were gorges to look up, and high bridges to look down, and snow summits through every opening, and lights and shadows playing all over ... We are now camped out. It is very hot and Elizabeth has gone off a little way to sketch ...

A day later, she added:

I am writing at 7.30 p.m. We walked nine miles today, taking our time and resting half-way up to this tiny village that's not even in our guidebook. It is a charming place, and the girl who waited on us says the English pass by, but never stay here. She and her younger sister are so glad to talk to us, and Elizabeth has given them some Gospels which they've promised to read ...

When they came to Göschenen, Fanny knew she had to write and describe it for the family at home.

We have come to a wee village, shut in by the wildest, most savage-looking heights, mostly topped with snow, awful rocks and a great avalanche gorge on one side, a wild valley narrow and solemn on the other side, shut in at the end by what looks like a very large glacier, which they say no one has ever yet crossed. We are close to a bridge over a very deep and narrow gorge, and about 100 yards[2] off we can get back into the Great St. Gotthard pass, very grand both up and down. And here we are going to spend Sunday! We cannot possibly get to church, and I really think it will be as good as going to church, just for once. We are 3,000 feet[3] high here. We made ourselves cosy little nests among the boulders and moss and had a small service together. Afterwards, each of us spent time alone, agreeing to meet mid-afternoon.

The guidebook described the next climb they had chosen, up the Furkahorn, as one demanding a guide. Elizabeth soon found them one, a kindly, fatherly-looking guide well acquainted with the Furkahorn and willing to take them up.

In Fanny's next letter she wrote:

There is no track up the Furkahorn ... our guide went first, feeling every step lest he should fall through. We followed his instructions, stepping exactly in his steps, but it is not at all like walking. Each step is a separate thing; you stand firm, take time to plant each foot, and if there are hidden

2. 91.4 metres.
3. 914.4 metres.

holes, the guide of course tumbles in first, and we stand still while he gets out and tries for a better footing. Sometimes we are up to our knees in snow. The view at the top was wonderful, but we could only stay a few minutes because, as our guide pointed out, most awful-looking clouds were gathering and quite all at once it began to sleet violently. Our guide took us down a longer way that was safer for descent, but not before we were suddenly wrapped in a cloud that made it so difficult to see that I was not sorry when we were down safely. The storm continued so fiercely that our innkeeper has had to shutter three of our windows, leaving only one on the sheltered side open for light.

Elizabeth, who had been listening to Fanny read her letter aloud, interrupted, 'Fanny, I am afraid you will frighten everyone at home, and they will be sending someone to look after us!'

Fanny added a line to her letter.

Seriously, however, I do not consider that we have done anything dangerous, and I mean to keep the promise I made about that.

'That should help,' she said.

Elizabeth groaned. Their wet clothes were drying and both were in their beds to keep warm. A few days after this, they met two famous guides whose names Fanny had read in the guidebook, and a third experienced Alpine climber. They were breakfasting at the little inn and talking about the largest snow avalanche any of them had seen before, 400 feet[4] wide!

---

4. 121.92 metres.

Only days ago, they had seen it coming and managed to get out of its way; in three seconds they saw it far below.

'We would have all most certainly have been killed,' one said. Fanny was thinking that was a true danger no one could have foreseen, not even such experienced guides. Only the best of guides would have known – the Lord Jesus, the perfect guide.

Not many days later, as they climbed with their guide, she did admit to Elizabeth, 'I think I must say that I may not be keeping my promise about danger, because there seems so much of it here. If we had slipped in some places it would have been no small thing; but I never feel giddy and I have a sure foot I am certain, and I don't feel nervous.'

Their guide, who had been watching them closely, told them later he'd been certain his two inexperienced climbers would not make the top, but as they got over the first snow and rocks, he changed his mind. He remarked that Fanny climbed like a chamois[5], a compliment!

Wherever they went, Fanny and Elizabeth took Gospel tracts and small New Testaments and some hymns from the supplies. So far, they had given out Christian materials to the girls who served them at the inns and others they met along the way. While Elizabeth had sat down with an eager group of children to talk to them, Fanny saw an old woman a little way off watching

5. Mountain goat.

her goats as she sat knitting, and went to sit by her. As they talked in German, the woman told Fanny that she thought of heaven and prayed God would show her how to get there. 'It would be so good to be with Jesus,' she said. Fanny was soon reading Romans 8 to her slowly and pointing to each line as she read. The woman followed and repeated the most comforting words. When they finished, Fanny marked the place and gave her the little book. As Fanny left, she saw that the woman was bent over the book, her knitting laid aside and the goats on their own.

It was one of the guides they met who surprised Fanny as they talked, by quoting from the book of Hebrews. 'But I thought no one here was allowed to read the Bible; that the priests forbid it,' Fanny said. She had heard this from a missionary that it was so in all of the Catholic Cantons throughout Switzerland.

'Yes, that is true,' he said, 'and my New Testament was a gift to me from a visiting English lady, but I did read it and have not stopped. There are others here who do the same now.' That night, Fanny told Elizabeth what the guide had said.

'How wonderful,' Elizabeth said, her dark eyes wide. 'I think he must be a believer or close to becoming one, and just think how a single gift of God's Word from a stranger may lead someone to Christ.'

'Oh, Elizabeth, if only we could wish and bring all of our Y.W.C.A. sisters here to give out the gospel all over these mountains, who knows how many might be brought to him! How I thank him for each opportunity we have had to spread his Word. And I meant to tell you, Elizabeth, that your idea to get the children to show you how well they can read, while their proud parents stand by listening to them, is a fine way for the parents to hear the good news too. So many in this area are afraid to take a Christian book because of the priests. But now we know that there are some like our guide friend who will even disobey the priests.'

'This trip has been all I could have dreamt of and more,' Elizabeth said, arranging her things for the next morning's early call.

Fanny laughed lightly. 'Yes, and I do think we both needed it. Isn't it good to be free of that old feeling of having to hurry, hurry to do all the things you need to do? It's like our youth has been renewed! Here we are, scrambling about, laughing, enjoying God's wonderful creation. And back home, neither of us could have walked more than a mile or two, but here we go nine miles and we're still ready for a challenge the next day.'

Elizabeth stretched and drew in a deep breath of night air blowing into their room. 'It is all true,' she said, 'except for those dreadful times when it was utterly impossible to sleep and we were so worn out the next day. Like the time we couldn't find a room and spent all night sitting up. I went everywhere looking for a room for us. Or worse, the time we got caught in that sudden storm and had to take shelter in that awful inn, remember that?'

'How could I forget such a night?' Fanny said, picturing it in her mind. 'Dirty beds on a dirty floor in a kitchen I don't have time to describe. Poor family. At least we had two wooden boxes to sit on all night.' Fanny suddenly laughed. 'Oh Elizabeth, you know that neither of us would have dared to be on that floor with everything crawling on it.' Both of them were laughing now at the remembered scene. The storm had finally stopped and they'd left at the first streak of dawn. When their laughter finally quietened, Fanny said, 'How good of the Lord to remind us that there are such places, and truly they could not begin to spoil the sights and joys he has given us day after day. Could we ever have imagined the wonders of his hand, or how he would give us the joy of spreading his light and love this way?'

Fanny and Elizabeth had decided they were becoming good climbers and could take on greater heights. Fanny especially felt stronger and fitter than ever. It was early July, and climbing even in snow made her so hot that on one climb she stopped to peel off her skirt and continued on in her petticoat! Elizabeth wasn't far behind in doing the same. They travelled as light as possible, even cutting out only the pages of the guidebook that they needed to carry. Now, even the hardest climbs were challenges they wanted to tackle, and did.

In one of her circular letters, Fanny wrote:

It is utterly impossible to write hymns here — there is not the remotest chance of one unless we have a spell of bad weather! You cannot think what it is: always something to look at or do — every step needs looking at, it is not like walking along a road, and imagine the ever-changing mountains and sky, the Alpine flowers! The only thing I could write about is Switzerland! Elizabeth and I get up before five and often before four. I think it is the best thing for me and I feel it is doing me so much good, refreshing my health and my mind.

While coming down into the Italian side of the Alps, they could see fields with vines and fruit trees below. 'It's just like something out of a book, every page new and beautiful!' Fanny exclaimed. And it was here that a mistake led them to see the most beautiful sunrise of all. They had ordered to be called at 3.00 a.m., thinking that would give their Italian host time to surely call them by four. When the call came and they got up, Fanny said, 'What a dark morning this is, Elizabeth.' They were dressed and ready to go down when Fanny looked at her watch. 'It was only 2.20 a.m.! Downstairs coffee waited, and a friend Elizabeth knew who was to climb with them to see Mont Blanc at sunrise. He warned them that once the sun rose over the shoulder of the mountain it would be a terribly hot walk, and they must leave at once.

At first, the three of them walked under stars with a cool breeze from Mont Blanc coming straight down to them. The dawn came with a few specks of pink and gold, and one little pale cloud about halfway up the mountain. But it was a sunrise like no other Fanny had ever seen. The sudden touch of rose-fire covered Mont Blanc, spreading the blazing rose-fire down to the small cloud. Fanny couldn't say a word. Elizabeth caught her breath and then said, 'It is the most heavenly thing upon earth.' There were no more words to describe it. In fifteen minutes it faded into the light of a common day. If they had been later they would have missed it! On the way back, Fanny could not help sharing her favourite mountain verse:

'Unto Thee, O God, do we give thanks, unto thee do we give thanks: for that thy name is near thy wondrous works declare.' [6]

'This has been the most wonderful trip I have ever taken, one I know we'll never forget,' Fanny said as they stood at the boat railing, watching the French shoreline fading from sight. The crossing was smooth, and the day still fine when she and Elizabeth arrived in England. Elizabeth's family were waiting near Maria and Fanny's brother, Frank, to welcome them home.

---

6. Psalm 75:1.

Full Surrender

Fanny did not go home directly to Leamington, but to Oakhampton. Her mother had gone to visit friends, and Miriam's whole family were away. Beautiful Oakhampton with its fields and gardens and sun room waited for her. The servants had been told to expect her and each of them knew her well, as she them. Calls of 'Welcome, welcome, Miss Frances!' greeted her as she stepped from the carriage. They could not do enough for her!

On Sunday after church, Fanny rested, and when she came downstairs for tea, dear old Miss Gundy set a large spread before her. 'Now, Miss Frances, you just eat all you can, but leave room for them apple turnovers you love.' Miss Gundy smiled broadly.

'Oh, Miss Gundy, you are taking such good care of me, and I can never resist your apple turnovers,' Fanny said.

'All of us are hoping you won't refuse to sing with us, seeing as how the Mistress ain't here tonight. On Sunday nights, we learn songs from *Songs of Grace and Glory* and *Havergal's Psalmody*. We learn a new hymn and tune each week and keep up the old ones too. And I tell you, Miss Frances, you will be pleased to hear the footman learns the bass of every one!'

Fanny was amazed! This was the first she had heard
about Miriam's musical evenings with the servants.
'You must tell the others that I can't think of anything
that I would enjoy more tonight than singing with all
of you,' she said. 'And, if you like, we could try a new
song to surprise Mrs. Crane with when she gets back.'
The young serving maid, Mary, who had just brought
in dessert and set it down, couldn't help saying, 'Oh,
please Miss, it would be lovely.' Fanny smiled. Nothing
would please her more than having a small hand in
Miriam's loving work with the servants.

Later that night, Fanny wrote in her journal how
well it had all gone, including the amazing footman's
bass! She knew all of Miriam's servants and had talked
with them about the Lord more than once. 'Miriam
should have heard them sing tonight,' she wrote. 'Even
dear old Miss Gundy sang her best. No one minded
any little faults. The words of the songs seemed the
very ones they wanted to sing from their hearts, and
they did!'

Afterwards, all of the servants in the little choir had
thanked her. Miss Gundy had tears in her eyes as she
left. 'It was so good to sing His praises,' Miss Gundy
said. Mary, the youngest of the maids, nodded her head
in agreement, and Fanny saw a tear slide down that
young face. Now Fanny felt tears in her own eyes as
she laid down her pen for the night. Her heart was full
with thanks for Miriam's little servants' choir. 'What a
sweet sound, Lord,' she whispered.

Back home at Leamington, Fanny stepped right into her old busy schedule, beginning at once with the St. Paul Church's voluntary choir she led. She was writing poems too, and sometimes found herself longing to share a new poem with her father. 'I will think about the good things, Lord,' she whispered. 'How good it is to write lines that tell about you, and how I pray they will reach someone's heart with your love, Lord.'

Soon it would be Christmas, and everywhere Fanny went, even among the poorest of the cottagers, it was a time for Christmas greetings and cheer. 'How I love visiting them,' she said to Maria. 'I can't count the many times the Lord Jesus makes me glad I went.' The weather had been cold, even for December, and Fanny was bringing a thick, warm shawl for one of the old women she loved to visit. Like so many poor widows, this woman had few comforts and Fanny was glad for her to have this shawl, one she liked but could do without. As Fanny wrapped the shawl around her thin shoulders, the old widow cried, 'Oh no! I seen you wear it often, and it's so fine, I canna take it.' Fanny gently persuaded her how much she wanted her to have it. 'Well, then, inasmuch,' the old woman said, smoothing the folds of the shawl. Fanny knew what she meant:

'Whatever we do for the least of God's children, it is just as if we did it for him.'[1]

---

1. Matthew 25:40.

Fanny left, thanking God for the joy he'd given her.

This was such a busy time of year, but as Christmas day grew closer, Fanny's mother grew less able to enjoy anything that reminded her of how Fanny's father would have been involved. Christmas was one of the highlights of the year for him. And this Christmas, the second one since his death, was an anniversary her mother could not face. Fanny feared her mother would be ill and asked Maria, who was helping at Winterdyne, if she could come home. Thankfully, Maria understood Fanny's need for help and came as soon as she could.

Christmas afternoon, Fanny wrote a greeting and a thank you to Elizabeth who was still at Winterdyne helping Ellen.

> *I must send you a line of Christmas greeting — I am so glad you are staying on at Winterdyne. I truly needed Maria's help with our mother. Christmas can be such a painful time for widows, and it seems as hard for my mother this year as it was last Christmas after my father's death. I'm glad for all the sympathy shown to lonely widows, but you and I and Maria know how lonely the heart can feel too when the joy of marriage seems not to be one we will ever know. I think we should like some sympathy too. But it helps me to think Jesus will pour his love into my heart, and I can trust his plans for me. Pray for me, dear one, and I for you in this ....*

Maria had come upstairs with a tea tray for the two of them. 'Mama is visiting with Miss Jenkins, and the two of them are quite happy to let me go,' Maria said putting the tray on the table next to Fanny's armchair. 'Now you must help me with all this or I shall not eat a bite!' she threatened.

Fanny was hungry and glad for Maria's company too. 'Maria, you are a marvel. Here I am in my room all day, and you are waiting on me. And you've had the full care of Mama for the last three days too.' Fanny sighed and took a bit of the thick barley soup Maria had brought. Under another covered dish were sausages, and next to it a dainty basket piled high with hot rolls. Fanny was sure that the covered dessert dish would hold some 'Astley' apple turnovers. 'Everything looks so good!'

Maria patted Fanny's arm and said, 'I love cooking and with only one servant in the house, I can.' She offered the rolls to Fanny, adding, 'Are you feeling better? You did give us a fright the other day. The doctor says it's just exhaustion and you need to rest.'

'I'm almost back to my old self,' Fanny said. 'And it's a good thing because there is so much I need to do. The choir needs to practice for the winter concert.'

Fanny kept a daily calendar when she could, and sometimes surprised even herself with how full a day could be. One day read:

Before 7.00 a.m. I was dressed, made my bed. Read two chapters in Romans. At 8.30 a.m. wrote to a publisher about a hymn, copied new hymn. Prayers and breakfast, 9.00 to 9:45 a.m. Consulted Mama about letters, calls and house errands, and dusted drawing-room. At 11:45 a.m. began copy of My Singing Lesson *for publisher; corrected proofs.'*

The rest of the day had been completely filled with fifteen minutes out for rest that evening at 6.45 p.m., and she hoped to write after that until tea at 7:30 p.m. Her days did always seem full.

In February, Fanny wrote to encourage a friend not to keep working without any rest or break, saying, '... sooner or later if you won't take care, you will find you must.' Fanny did mean to follow her own advice, but often resting time turned into writing time. She wrote to Elizabeth of one of her hymns to be published in a magazine:

> *It is so good to think that people who will never see* Songs of Grace and Glory *may read this in a magazine that reaches 50,000 people ....*

Fanny worked hard, but her slight build and fragile health soon gave way to utter exhaustion, a feeling of weakness close to fainting. Sometimes fever and aching followed. She could no longer direct the St. Paul Church choir and gave it up. There were no new poems or songs, and what she had been working on now sat idle. She did manage letters when she could. Her mother reminded her, 'Fanny, you must be more careful and rest. The illness you suffered as a child has left your health more delicate, dear.'

'You are right, Mama,' she said. 'But it's so hard not to have any ongoing work for the Lord.'

'Well, we must trust him, dear, and rest,' her mother said.

Later, in a letter to a friend, she wrote things that she could say so much easier in writing. 'I have been feeling very down,' she wrote, 'and I hope humbled … I feel like everyone is doing more and better than myself … Pray for me, that I may really learn all he is teaching me ….'

As she slipped the letter into an envelope, a Bible verse she had learned came to her: 'He will be very gracious unto thee at the voice of thy cry.'[2]

She didn't see or feel how God would be gracious, but she did believe his Word was true.

By summer, Maria had plans to visit North Wales, and Fanny went with her. In a letter to Elizabeth, she wrote:

> I can't tell you how many answers to prayer in little things we have had here; it's truly marvellous. I am feeling so trim, really first-rate, and find the walks here are not difficult for me. Wales is beautiful but in a different way from Switzerland, like a forget-me-not is beside a rose, both lovely in their own way. I can climb Snowdon to the top (where I am sitting writing to you), all its paths up are so easy! I have had 600 letters between January and July to answer and many proofs of poems and leaflets and songs to work on besides. I am so thankful how good Wales has been for me. Maria and I have given out gospel literature too, but I will wait to tell you more about that when we get back. We leave Wales at the end of July.

---

2. Isaiah 30:19.

By November, Fanny was writing her new book *Under the Surface* and Ellen had invited her to Winterdyne for a 'get-away'. Ellen had come in to see how she was doing with the new book and brought tea with her. 'How is it coming?' she asked.

Fanny was glad for the break and the lovely tea. 'Well, I am getting on rapidly with it. There will be just ninety poems and hymns, and the book will be quite a bit larger than *Ministry of Song*.' Fanny took a sip of tea. 'Mmm. Oh, and I just received a letter pressing me to publish my *Hints to Lady Mission Workers*.' Fanny was a member of the Christian Women Workers. 'Our loving Father has given me so much success this year with my pen and opportunities to speak for him! The London publishers are happy with my translation into English of six beautiful songs by Franz Abt.'

'Oh Fanny, that's wonderful,' Ellen said. 'But you must take care not to overtax yourself now.'

'I am doing that, really, Ellen. You see how I keep out of everybody's way here at Winterdyne. I decline every evening invitation, so people catch me if they can in the afternoon.'

'Yes, and Giles and I are glad to be of help that way,' Ellen said and giggled. 'Just think of us as two old dragons keeping everyone from your door. But you know how wonderfully you have been refreshed and brought back to health when you spend time away in Switzerland or Wales. I hope you won't say no to those invitations.'

'Oh, Ellen, the very thought of the hills of Wales and the mighty Alps, getting so close to God's creation, makes me long to go. I could not refuse if I wanted to,' she said. After many months of hard work and longing for even a week away from proofs, Fanny went with Mr. and Mrs. Snepp to Switzerland. It was the one trip for Fanny where she nearly lost her own life and the lives of all those roped together with her.

Their little group of four had been glissading[3] down from Mont Blanc. Fanny was roped next to the guide, Mr. and Mrs. Snepp roped behind them. Fanny loved glissading. But then at one spot she was a bit careless and slipped, taking the guide with her. Below was a dark abyss, and the rope they were attached to spun them rapidly down a very steep incline to a sheer precipice below. Instantly Mr. Snepp threw himself onto his back and dug his heels in the snow. It was the only way he could possibly save all four of them. Thanking God, Fanny and the guide soon recovered their footing. Fanny was freed of the rope for the rest of the way down. It did not take away her joy in glissading, but she would not forget this day.

Back from Switzerland, Fanny was soon busy again with the works she loved, including helping with the choir. She wrote to her Y.W.C.A. sisters,

I wish I could have come to the last meeting. I have so much to tell you all. If I'd been keeping a diary this summer, it would be just a record of answers to prayer. I know you would

---

3. Sliding down a steep slope of snow or ice, typically on the feet.

> be encouraged to hear how wonderfully God has answered
> one of your members, me! So, to all of you my love, and
> remember, he is the same God, rich to all that call to him.

It was almost the end of 1873 when something wonderful
happened that changed Fanny's whole life. She was
visiting Winterdyne, and one day a letter came for her
with a tiny book enclosed. The title was *All for Jesus*. Fanny
read it carefully. The little book told of a Christian way
of life that Fanny hadn't known before. She wrote to the
author, telling her she longed to know more. 'I know I
love Jesus and love to serve him, but giving everything to
Jesus seems to be so much more,' she wrote. In the days
that followed Fanny came to see what that 'more' meant,
and with it a blessing such as she had never known. She
wrote to Maria to tell her the glad news.

> I know now that there must be a full surrender to the Lord
> of our lives! I've just given myself to him, and I trust him
> to keep me. I know we all sin, but we never have to be five
> minutes away from being cleansed by him. I'm simply
> believing his promise and trusting that he will help us do
> what without him we could not do. I feel as if the shadows
> are gone and I'm standing in the sunlight at last!

Fanny was still at Winterdyne when she wrote a hymn
called *From Glory unto Glory* and, handing it to Henry to
read, said, 'There! I could not have written this before.'
Now, on all her visits, she longed for whole households
to know with her the goodness of the Lord. It was that
kind of visit that led to another hymn, one she would
live to carry out.

Fanny was invited for a five-day visit to a friend's home. There were ten guests in the house, some not Christians that she had been praying for, and some who were Christians, but not happy ones. No one seemed to have an interest in deeper things. Fanny longed for these friends to know the Lord Jesus in a real way and prayed that the Lord would work in all of them. Before the week was up he did, and Fanny found herself talking of the Lord to each one in ways she could never had done alone. By the end of the week, all had come closer to the Lord. Fanny was so happy that the last night of her visit she couldn't sleep. Soon words came to her heart and she wrote them down in a hymn. Lines came like:

Take my life and let it be
Ever, only, Lord for Thee.

Among them were two that went:

Take my voice, and let me sing,
Always, only, for my King.

From that day, she chose to sing only words she really felt and loved and knew would please the Lord. One day, after she'd sung at a garden party, a young man came to talk to her. Fanny began a light conversation with him, but almost at once he turned to things about faith, his own lack of it, and how her song had moved him. Fanny never knew what happened to the young man after that day, but he had left deeply moved by their talk.

In Fanny's own copy of her *Ministry of Song* book, she often wrote the stories behind the hymns. A single sentence from her father's sermon became the song *This Same Jesus*. Another hymn came on New Year's night as the bells were ringing and Maria quoted her New Year's motto, 'As thy days, so shall thy strength be.' It was the same with hymn after hymn coming to her from something she saw or read or heard.

Her works were being widely read and used and Fanny was continually adding to collections like *Songs of Grace and Glory*. With every change, came letters to publishers, proofs to read and edit and all that went with writing. Fanny was expecting a letter from America with a cheque for £35 from an American publisher. She also hoped to hear that her book *Bruey* was doing well and *Under the Surface* also. Instead, the American publisher informed her that his company had collapsed in the widespread crash of financial markets. Fanny had given him in writing a promise to publish in America only with him. It was a great loss, both of money and her hope to be known in America, at least for a long time to come. Fanny had been writing a letter to Mrs. Snepp and put it down to open the one from America. She turned to finish the letter to her friend and wrote:

> *I am trusting in his will for me in everything, and learning the wonder of finding myself saying, 'Thy will be done', not with a sigh, but with a song! All for Jesus really means all, not halfway, and it's so good to put it all in his hands.*

'Kept'

When Fanny's stack of mail came with a letter from her niece, Constance, she opened it at once. 'So, dear Aunt Fanny, will you come with me to Switzerland in September? Elizabeth and two other school friends, Margaret and Bessie, will join us there.' It was just what Fanny knew she needed, a month of refreshing walks and climbs in the Alps. She did need rest and a quiet place far from interruptions to write, and in the heart of God's mighty mountains, was the very place! For the first month of the trip, her plan was to enjoy walking, climbing, resting and whatever ways the Lord might give her to serve him on her holiday. The second month she would make writing the first thing instead of idleness. After a grand month of climbs and visits and a glorious sunset on the Faulhorn, Fanny wrote her mother,

It was like standing midway between heaven and earth surrounded with clouds, then rifts of colours, and suddenly a burst of blazing sunshine all around us, a perfect paradise of golden and rosy slopes and summits ....

At the end of it they had stood on the mountain and sung a song of praise.

'I will miss you all, and think of you having adventures on the rest of your trip, dears,' Fanny said as she watched her nieces and the others, including Elizabeth, leave. 'Now,' she told herself, 'it's writing for me!' Fanny smiled. She had a whole month ahead of her here in Switzerland to get plenty of fresh air half the day and write for four to five hours the rest of the day. In her next circular letter home to her anxious mother she wrote:

I am doing it all in moderation, and it is so good to have no other calls on my time or strength. Last month's rest has made me feel as if nature got inside me and spring-cleaned everything, ready for a fresh new start. And I am so glad now to be staying in one place. There are opportunities to speak for Jesus and they just keep coming. I thank him for these. The other day when I sat down to write The Thoughts of God, *I was expecting it to be one of my best poems. Suddenly, a question came to mind: would you be just as willing to do any little bit of work for him, something for little children or poor people, something simple that others might not see and praise like this poem? Mama, I was so happy to say (and I know he heard me) that I really wanted to do what he chose for me to do, whatever it might be. I had only written four lines of the poem when someone came to my deserted little hiding place near a little mountain stream, and soon we were talking about Jesus and the good news in the little book in front of us. Before I knew it two young folks joined us, and after they had all left, a young lad and his sister came to ask if I would talk to them too. Clearly, Jesus had heard me say I wanted, more than anything else, to do whatever he chose for me to do, and he chose to send these 'little ones'. It seems so clear that Jesus took my really wanting to do whatever he chose for me and sent them to me! I know he guides me, and Mama dear, I am taking him at his Word in everything, so I know his promise to keep all I give of myself to him is true.*

Now, let me tell you what I have written here and what I am going to write:

- Our Swiss Guide. *An article for* Sunday Magazine *to talk about Jesus our true guide.*

- For Charity. *A song ready to publish.*

- Enough. *A short sacred poem.*

- How Much for Jesus? *A little true story for children.*

- True Hearted. *New Year's Address in verse for the Y.W.C.A. for January 1875.*

- Tiny Tokens. *A small poem for GoodWords.*

- Precious Things. *A poem.*

- A Suggestion. *A short paper for Home Words.*

- The Precious Blood of Jesus. *A hymn.*

- The Thoughts of God *(which I told you about).*

- Shining for Jesus. *Verses to my nieces and nephews at Winterdyne.*

- New Year's Wishes *by Caswell's (an artist friend). Request for a very pretty card.*

These are all written and copied, and done with. Next week, God willing, I shall set about what I have long wanted to do: Little Pillows, *thirty-one short papers as a little book for twelve years olds; a short easily remembered Bible text to go to sleep upon for each night of the month, with a*

*page or two of simple, practical thoughts about it, such as
a little girl might read every night while having her hair
brushed. I think this will take me about a fortnight to write
and arrange for press, adding probably a verse or two of a
hymn at the end of each of the little papers. I think I shall
get in three other little poems and a little article for the
Dayspring. If I could manage three months every year in a
Swiss or Welsh valley, I should keep my publisher going ....*

At the end of September, Fanny wrote her last letter
home.

I have finished not only Little Pillows, *but also* Morning
Bells *to go with it, both ready for press. I hope they will
be really helpful to some of his little ones. Shall I give
you a peek inside* Little Pillows? *It starts like this: How
Little Pillows came to be written. A little girl was away
from home on a week's visit. We will suppose her name was
Ethel. The first night, when she was tucked up in bed, and
just ready for a good-night kiss, I said, 'Now, shall I give
you a little pillow?'*

*Ethel lifted her head to see what was under it and said,
'I have got one, Auntie!'*

*'It was another sort of pillow that I meant to give you;
I wonder if you will like it?'*

*Ethel realised that it was not a pillow to sleep on, but
she still did not understand, and so she laughed and said,
'Do tell me at once, Auntie, what you mean; don't keep me
waiting to guess!'*

*Then I told her that, just as we want a soft pillow
to lay our heads down upon at night, our hearts want a
pillow too, something to rest upon, some true, sweet word
that we might go to sleep upon happily and peacefully.*

And that it was a good plan always to take a little text for your pillow every night. So she had one that night and the next night. The third night, I was prevented from coming up till long after Ethel should have been asleep. But there the bright eyes peeping out robin-redbreast fashion, and a reproachful little voice said, 'Auntie, you have not given me a little pillow tonight!'

'Then do you really care about having the little pillows given you, Ethel?'

'Oh, of course I do!' was the answer. She did not seem to think there could possibly be any doubt about it. Certainly the way in which she said that 'of course!' showed that she had no doubt about it!

'So it seemed that perhaps other little ones would like to have a 'little pillow' put ready for them every night. For even little hearts are sometimes very weary and want something to rest upon; and a happy little heart, happy in the love of Jesus, will always be glad to have one of his own sweet words to go to sleep upon ....

I think this letter is quite long enough, so I will just give you a tiny bit of the opening of one my favourite little pillows, God's Care. *He that keeps you will not slumber.*

Sometimes, little children wake in the night and feel lonely, and a little bit afraid. This is not because of the darkness; for if others are with them, talking and moving about, they do not mind it at all. But it is the stillness, the strange silence when everybody is fast asleep. Everybody? No! ... (You will have to wait to read the rest when I get home, which will be quite soon now.)'

Fanny had decided on one last long walk, actually one that would take her three days of hiking, resting and stopping in small Swiss inns to reach the train at Montreux. She had sent her luggage ahead of her by post, a very Swiss thing to do. Only last week at dinner, Madame Treina had apologised for serving only chicken, because the beef had not come by post.

Fanny could have gone to Montreux by carriage or by rail, but she thought the walk would do her good after so much writing. Only once did she almost regret her choice, at least at first. It wasn't the small inn, where she was sure the floors had not been washed in a year, maybe two, and the bed was one she was glad to forget; it was something that she had never expected to find in Switzerland! The rudest, most angry, unkind serving girl in a rough inn where the weather gave Fanny no choice but to stay the night.

A tall, bold, rough girl of twenty-five or so let Fanny in. 'Yes, you can have a room when it's ready; not before. Here, in here!' She led Fanny to a dark, dirty room with tables and benches and left her there, shutting the door behind her. It got quite dark and when five or six men came in, the girl brought a candle, and the men sat down at a table to smoke. Fanny asked if her room was ready and was told, 'No, you must wait!' Fanny waited nearly an hour before the girl came for her. The room was bare except for a barley-straw bed and no pillow. Just as Fanny was going to bed, a sharp, angry rap at the door and a hard rattling of the handle came along with the girl's demanding voice, 'Are you going to burn the candle all night? How soon are you going to put it out, I should like to know!' Fanny answered meekly and went to bed. In the morning she asked God if he would shut the girl's mouth and open hers. When Fanny asked for coffee, the girl said rudely, 'Can't have coffee till it's made.' There was no butter, but there was bread for the coffee. When Fanny finished, she went close to the girl, looked into her angry eyes, and placed a hand on her arm.

Gently, Fanny said, 'You are not happy: I know you are not.' Fanny went on to tell her how she'd seen her sadness even when the girl joked with the men, and how Fanny had prayed for her last night. She told her about Jesus and what he could do for her. The girl tried hard not to cry, and Fanny knew it was only God's hand that made her listen. Fanny gave her the little book *A Saviour for You* in French and the girl promised to read it, thanking her over and over. Before she left, Fanny also talked to the girl's old mother. Surely God had meant for Fanny to be at this very inn last night! She left, thanking him and asking for his mercy on the poor girl.

Fanny left Switzerland glad that she now did feel stronger than when she'd first arrived. By the time she arrived in Leamington from a visit with cousins in London, something had changed. Fanny came home shivering and feverish and quickly became worse. Somewhere along the way she had picked up typhoid fever. Her mother's care, trained nurses and all that the doctor could do, failed to stop the attack. By mid-

November, Fanny lay close to death. Maria stayed by her bedside, resting only when others came to take her place. Family and servants, friends and all over the country people who knew her writings prayed and pleaded for her life. Special prayer meetings were held, and when Fanny was restored, there was great thanksgiving. It was weeks later that Fanny told Maria how she had been in such pain at first that she could not help groaning and longing for the poultices to ease the agony.

'Maria, I did not think of death as a dark valley, I only thought that he was coming for me and I should see my King. And when I was recovering and then fell ill again, I could not even pray, or think, but only say, "Lord Jesus, I am so tired!" And then he brought to my mind, "Rest in the Lord, be silent to him" and I felt peace and love. Oh Maria, how he keeps us in his hand even when we can't pray or do a thing to help ourselves.'

In mid-January, Fanny seemed a little recovered and the doctor suggested a change of air at Winterdyne might do her good. A few days later, she was ill again for many weeks.

In the hallway, Ellen was about to send for a nurse, but the servants Fanny had cared for, taught and loved at Winterdyne, begged to sit up with Miss Frances, who they said 'was no trouble at all, so patient, so thankful, so considerate.' In April, Fanny was able to be moved to Oakhampton where Miriam and the servants Fanny had ministered to there waited to do all they could for her. As the Winterdyne servants gathered round to say goodbye, Fanny thanked them for all their kindness in her illness and said, 'Remember, God's promises are for each of you; faith is just holding out your hand and taking them. It is what I am learning every day; it makes me happy, and I want all of you to be always happy, trusting in the Lord Jesus.'

At Oakhampton, there were still months of battle with recovery and relapses. Fanny could do little but obey doctor's orders. At last, she had gone from being carried downstairs to the parlour to walking with crutches, until finally she could truly say she was no longer ill, though she still needed much rest. She was resting in an armchair near the fireplace, sewing lace onto a small garment for the mission box while Miriam and Maria cut and sewed other little garments. Maria looked up from her work to ask, 'Fanny dear, we've talked so much about how faithful the Lord was all through these many months of illness, answering our prayers and keeping you safe. But what was it you said about waiting? I am trying to remember your words.'

Fanny stopped her work for a moment. 'I think I said that when all I could do was wait for whatever Jesus would choose for me, I found out that "Waiting for him, is waiting with him, and that makes all the difference."'

Fanny smiled and took up her work. 'I'm glad to be able to work again. I can truly say, I am quite satisfied to do a half-day's work if he pleases. I have plenty of proof that he can make half an hour's work worth a whole day's if he will!' She had come upon a little poem that said just what she felt and so shared it:

> I am not eager, bold, or strong,
> All that is past;
> I'm ready not to do,
> At last, at last.
> My half-day's work is almost done,
> 'Tis all my part:
> I bring my patient God
> A patient heart.

God's Half-Timer

Fanny was home in Leamington with her mother, well again, but still could only do a little; write for an hour or two, see one or two people, sing one song, go to church once on Sunday and rest most of the day after church. She wrote to a friend, 'I am working a little, I think the workers in the factory call it 'a half-timer' … but it has been the most precious year of my life to me … proving the truth of Jesus' promise …"When you pass through the waters I will be with you."[1] Jesus' faithfulness is so real!' When the flood waters came again it was not illness this time.

Maria, who came often to check on Fanny and their mother, had just come to visit, and Fanny, hearing her voice, came flying down the stairs from her study. 'Oh, Maria,' she cried, 'it's done! I'm finally free to write a book!' In her hand was a large roll of papers, ready for the post.

'I'm so glad, Fanny, you've been working so long and hard on this appendix for *Songs of Grace and Glory*. And you must admit, it has really tired you.'

'It has taken all spring to compose quite new tunes to some hymns, and there were many others that

1. Isaiah 43:2.

needed careful revision, the kind of work that is tiring, but now it's done! The new music is finished and all the revisions, ready for the press.' It was one week later that Fanny received news she could never have imagined!

'Messrs. Henderson's premises were burned down this morning, about 4.00 a.m. We fear the whole of the stereotypes of your musical edition were destroyed, as they were busy printing it. It will be many days before the debris will be cool enough to see how the stereotype plates stand.' More news told her that, 'Your musical edition has been totally destroyed.' The worst part for Fanny was that this time she hadn't made a copy, not even a list of the tunes! Every chord of her own would need to be reproduced, as well as the chords of anyone else she'd revised for the appendix. She had not even kept a note to herself on most of the new work she had done, work that had taken her so long.

In a note to Elizabeth, she wrote: '... So I must just patiently rewrite my own tunes from memory, and I am hoping against hope that the proofs may be got through by August and I can go to Switzerland with Maria, which would probably do us both great good. Pray that I will do what seems like drudgery to me now, patiently, and have health enough for it. He has more to teach me! I have been so eager to finish *Songs of Grace and Glory*, and he is giving me the opportunity to do it over again more patiently and make it 'a willing service' this time, which it was not before ....'

It wasn't long before Fanny wrote another little note to Elizabeth: 'I need to tell you how gracious he has been to me. I thought this would be a useless spring with no serving anyone but in the last three days I have had notes telling me of times I was of real use and blessing to someone, none of which I would have guessed was happening. Now, isn't this enough to make one's heart overflow with praise? It is a sweet lesson of trust and simple dependence on him ...' The work was finally done, just as a request came from a London Missions worker for a leaflet based on Fanny's hymn *I could not do without Thee*. The leaflets were for workers to give out. Fanny wrote *I could not do without Him* and it was printed and also published in *HomeWords* magazine which went to 300,000 homes. Copies also went to the mission's work in America.

Elizabeth was going to the mission field! Fanny wrote to her at once:

> *Dear Elizabeth, I feel so solemnly glad about all this; I am more and more a 'cumberer'[2] so that I am really glad when others are able to do more service. You will be off to India, so far away, I will miss you and so will be both glad and sad at the same time! Going with the Zenana Mission will be so good; I do love their work. I shall long to hear that the Lord has made the way clear, and set before you an open door ....*

Fanny had dreamed of being a missionary and though it was not possible for her, she had just received news

---

2. A person or thing that takes up space or gets in the way.

from Punjab that *Morning Bells* and *Little Pillows* were going to be translated into Hindustani, and were already used in mission schools! The little books were also going to France to be published by the Religious Tract Society of France; and someone in high places was going to give them to all the royal children! Her publisher, Nisbet, had started with printing 4,000 of each book, but in seven weeks had to reprint them to keep up with the requests for them. Another short work, *Five Benefits* which she wrote for Caswell publishers, had to be reprinted four times in four weeks, the demand was so great! Sharing the good news in a note to Miriam, Fanny wrote:

> It seems to me that whenever I cannot do my own work and have to leave it entirely to God, he takes it up and does a good deal more for me than I should have done for myself, like sending my songs and books and writings to places I could never go. He did this too when I asked him not to let the Irish Society work of collecting suffer because of my illness. He brought so many to help with my collections and do even more that it was wonderful!

When an invitation came to sing at a concert in her brother Frank's church, Fanny accepted. She asked too if she could visit the nearby infirmary, and there she sang for the patients, read, prayed and spoke to each one, promising those who asked her to come back that she would. When Fanny went back, one woman who the day before had looked so distressed, now looked glad to see her. Though she was still suffering, she said to Fanny, 'I've left it all with him now, and oh it's so beautiful!' Another thanked Fanny, saying, 'The words God gave you to say to me have lifted me straight up into sunlight.' Still another had put her trust in the Lord Jesus. 'It was so good,' Fanny told Miriam, 'to see those dear ones who wanted to hear the good news of Jesus.' Back at Oakhampton, under Fanny's direction and Miriam's, the servants picked flowers from the large gardens, tied them in lovely little bouquets and attached the little cards Fanny wrote for each one, 300 for hospital patients. They were sent with Fanny's prayer that he would use them wherever they went.

It wasn't long before Fanny was packing again! Almost finished with her bag, she took the neatly folded blouse her mother handed her next to tuck in. 'Mama, just think our dear Maria is finally going with me for a good rest in Switzerland. She needs it so much, and I will be glad of it too. I just wish you were able to come, but I am glad you will be at the seashore and with friends who will love you and see that you do rest and enjoy your time.'

'Yes, child, and you take care that you do the same with your sister,' her mother said. 'I know that no argument could keep you from your beloved mountains, and God has always given you much joy there. I enjoy rereading the circular letters you always sent on your trips, now that I have them all back again.' Fanny smiled and gave her mother a gentle hug.

All of her sisters, Ellen, Miriam, and Maria, loved serving the Lord from the days their own mother and dear father had taught them by word and example. But it was Maria, unmarried, who found her way to the poor in workhouses, cottages, supporting missions work, teaching children, helping and loving and telling the good news of Jesus everywhere she went. Dear Maria, Fanny thought, dark-haired, dark-eyed, plainer a bit than Ellen and Miriam and now thinner than Fanny thought she should be, had sat by her bedside night and day through Fanny's worst times of pain and fever, always on call. But now, Fanny was going to go on holiday in Switzerland and this time Maria was going to come with her!

They were in Switzerland and had rested for three weeks when both Maria and Fanny were able to witness to a group of peasant girls and a local priest. Fanny sang and taught the girls a song she'd written in French, asking for their help as a little choir. She had written out a copy for the girls to fix its truth on their memory. Maria gave them a short Bible study on Romans 6:23 in French, then prayed. Maria asked the priest if she might borrow a French Bible, and asked him to see if her French verses were correct. He was very polite, and Maria went on to tell him how happy she was in Christ, and what was the secret of peace and joy. He listened and did not disagree, but she could not get him to talk more. They left by carriage and soon had the driver and passengers singing Fanny's new song in French. But even these little efforts seemed to be having an effect on Fanny. It had been thirteen months since she had been cured from her illness, but she had nothing like her former strength now. The three weeks any other time in the Alps would have put Fanny in tip-top fitness, but not this time! Even on the freshest of Swiss mornings she felt up to 'nothing'. This trip, she would rest more!

One Sunday, at a lovely restful guesthouse, Fanny felt led to play the piano in the large room, and was surprised that several asked her to sing after dinner for the many guests. 'Pray for me, Maria,' she said, 'that I may give the King's message in song and that it might reach some hearts.' Many came to thank her, but Fanny left quickly, trusting God would work in hearts.

Everywhere they went, it seemed there was what Fanny called 'happy work', telling others of her joy in Jesus, sharing the good news that was for them too. Maria smiled to hear Fanny's cheerful voice, her laughter too as she reached out to others. In Lauterbrunnen they stayed in a pension[3] in full view of the Jungfrau and Silberhorn. The mountains Fanny so loved! They were the only ones in the pension and warmly welcomed. They had no idea that their hosts would turn out to be kinder than they could have expected, when a simple walk caught Maria and Fanny in a downpour. Fanny's chill turned into fever

---

3. In France and some other countries — a relatively cheap boarding house.

and serious illness that kept them in the pension for the next month.

One morning, Maria found Fanny lying against the soft down pillows piled behind her, her Bible in her hand. 'Oh Maria, this is just what I needed. Listen: 2 Chronicles 32:8 says, "The people rested themselves upon the words of Hezekiah king of Judah." I will take it as my "little pillow", to rest my own heart on.'

After a day of suffering pain more than usual, she had fallen asleep, and a little while later awakened, saying, 'I have a new song, Maria.'

Fanny softly sang a bit of the first line, 'I take this pain, Lord Jesus,' before adding, 'It's about trusting him even with our pain. How could we look up to Jesus and say, "No, Lord, I do not trust you in everything?"'

It was October before Fanny could leave for home. In a note to a friend, Fanny wrote:

> *I meant to write this past month and then go home. God has chosen otherwise for me. I must put off any book writing ... How glad I am that our work is not measured by how much of it there is, or how good it seems, but just on the Lord Jesus, blessing ....*

Fanny remembered a curious thing she had almost forgotten, something she'd seen in Miriam's conservatory.

As Fanny had watched, the gardener cut off every bunch from a splendid vine. She learned that he had been training it for twelve years and never let it bear even one bunch of fruit, and now its main stem was 200 feet[4] long

---

4. 60.96 metres.

and 400 feet[5] long with its branches. That spring, he had pruned off 1,000 bunches! 'And what do you expect it to bear by and by?' Fanny had asked.

'Four hundredweight[6] of grapes, and please God, if I live to manage it, in two years this will be the finest vine in the county.' He had much patience, fourteen years with this vine! Fanny thanked the Lord Jesus, the wisest, best of all vine-keepers, for his patient, faithful work in her. She might not understand, but she did trust him and his Word! She had a precious little pillow to rest her heart on: his Word!

On the train ride home from Switzerland, Fanny, whose eyes had been closed, suddenly sat upright, and said, 'Maria, I see exactly what I am to write: I can write a little book, *My King*. Quickly, she said what each of the thirty-one days' writings would be, all of them about the Kingship of Jesus, with questions to answer, like: 'Why has God made Jesus King?'

Fanny's little book was published, and, though she had written it with no intention that men would read it, they did, and one well-known British preacher, Charles H. Spurgeon, wrote to thank her for its help. Fanny wrote four more in what was soon called, 'The Royal Series':

Royal Commandments, morning thoughts;

Royal Bounty, evening thoughts on the good things God provides;

5. 121.92 metres.
6. 203 kilograms

Loyal Responses — thirty-one poems based on Scripture, and finally

Royal Invitation, written especially for unbelievers.

Home at last, not ill, though tired, Fanny was glad to do whatever the Lord had for her to do. Almost at once, she sat down to write to Elizabeth and tell her all that had happened.

> *... and wait. Going to India was so right, and you are doing great things there for God. And I less and less. Everybody is so sorry for me, except me! But I know that the same peace he will give you in work will be mine in waiting. You know how my nature wants to be busy, and this waiting is really from him. It gives me joy to know that the King's servants are always really on duty, even while some can only stand. Pray for me as I for you ....*

Slowly, Fanny's strength returned, but sadly the mother who had become so dear to her was now ill. It was a spring morning in May 1878 and her mother had been unconscious for days now, when she suddenly awoke and recognised Fanny, who was kneeling by her. She smiled sweetly in that final moment of her life. Her stepmother was buried in Astley churchyard with the words:

> *She rests where her loved ones rest, and joins the throng,*
> *of them who see the Lamb, and sing that endless song.*

It was time now to close the Leamington home for good. 'I'd forgotten how much jewellery is here,' Fanny said, holding up one of her necklaces. In fact all of mine, my whole jewellery cabinet, must go to the Church

Missionary House. Whatever money they get from the sale will be well used in the work.'

'Are you sure you want to give it all away?' Maria asked.

Fanny was already setting aside a single locket with the only picture of her little niece, Evelyn, and the ring given to her after Evelyn's death. She chose two more brooches and the ring she had hoped to give little Evelyn. 'There, these I will keep, and send money to cover them to the mission.'

Maria shook her head and then smiled; she knew well what a joy it was for Fanny to give all she could to the Lord's work.

Finally, the packing was over! On the last evening at Leamington, Fanny sent for a number of night-school boys and gave them each baskets of books, maps, a magic lantern and things she had put aside for each.

'Shall we have some singing time together?' she asked them. Soon the room filled with a song she had written, *Tell it out*, and then others she had written just for them. Tears filled Maria's eyes as Fanny lovingly spoke to these boys she loved so much, and prayed for them before they left.

When it was time to join Maria in her little house in Mumbles, Wales, Fanny's first words were: 'I wanted so to come here with you, Maria.' She was so tired and glad to be in Maria's little Welsh retreat, that for days Fanny just rested. The sea air, the gentle walks at low tide, searching the little pools for sea anemones and watching the ocean waves, the sailing vessels coming into the harbour all touched Fanny with delight, and she could feel her tiredness disappearing. Even the great St. Bernard dogs and her pet kittens seemed all part of her healing. She had always loved animals, and easily slipped them into stories for children. She delighted too in talking to the Mumbles lighthouse keeper, who gladly shared his stories with her. Fanny studied the nautical almanac and learned all she could from the keeper too.

In her little study, 'the workshop', Fanny and Maria hung pictures of the snow-topped Alps and others that Fanny loved. There was one of the Astley church and the fields she'd roamed with her little dog, Flora, and her father's picture near it. The walls were quite filled with pictures, and near the door was Fanny's motto, 'For Jesus' sake only'. Her library was small but held books on science, geology, poetry, the classics, and biographies of godly people she admired, and her Hebrew Bible and Greek New Testament. Fanny still had her favourite chair from the Astley rectory, one older than herself. But now she had an 'American typewriter' next to her desk, a machine that Maria could often hear clicking rapidly as she worked when she should have been resting.

Fanny read her Bible by 7.00 a.m. in summer and by 8.00 a.m. in winter, and on bitterly cold mornings, Maria urged her to put her feet near the fire. 'I really need to study at my desk, dear, it's so much easier to make notes and connect verses,' Fanny said.

Fanny knew enough too about carpentry to make herself a stand for her harp-piano, and here she wrote melodies to her hymns for the book she was writing, *Loyal Responses*, and a song, *Loving all Along*. From one window in her room she could see the Bay of Caswell with its rocks and sunsets from a small sofa nearby. From the south window she saw the sea, and near that window placed an easy chair and a small table next to it.

In a letter to Elizabeth, she wrote,

> *I don't think I ever felt more thankful and glad for anything than on reaching this quiet little nest. God so graciously and perfectly met our special need ....*

Soon enough, this restful time for her began filling up, especially with letters and requests of all kinds. Many were letters from strangers, more than she and Maria could answer. Some begged Fanny to write things like hymns for special New Year services, cards for mourners, a new set of *Marching Orders* (to go with others she had already written). Others wanted poems to go with pictures, prayer, sympathy and counsel! She could not count the number of people who asked her to revise their manuscripts, sheets of music, proofs and add her opinion and how to get an article into a magazine. One, the strangest of all, was an apology to Fanny from someone who had been printing her poems with another author's name! Almost daily, music proofs came that needed many hours of careful revision. Fanny wrote as kindly and cheerily as she could, encouraging wherever she could, answering letters from friends often long after getting them, thankful when at last she could.

There was work of another kind too that Fanny felt led to do, the kind she loved to do, and couldn't have resisted if she tried. It was the cottages near them, and Fanny began visiting them. She longed to have a Bible study too and soon had one going at Mumbles. The class filled the room each time, and Fanny even thought of having them meet at the schoolroom nearby as the class grew larger. Fanny loved her class, but by the end of a month she felt her old exhaustion returning. 'You need to give up the class, dear, and rest,' Maria urged. For a few weeks, Fanny was too ill to do anything.

Slowly, her strength returned, and Fanny began to take little walks. One morning, at breakfast, she said, 'It's so delightful being here, and I think God gave me the wish to come. We won't understand the puzzling parts of God's leading us, but it's like what poor Howells said to me on the cliffs yesterday. He was dressed in his old threadbare coat, and he told me how good the Lord was to him, and said, "He's been particularly good to me!" I've known his goodness too, even through "the puzzling times".'

Maria's large, dark eyes pooled with tears. 'That dear man. I must make some Astley turnovers for you to take when you visit next.' Maria wiped her eyes and added, 'Having you here is his goodness to me.'

'And you are one of His mercies to me,' Fanny said. 'And when I think back to last summer when we saw that glorious sunrise blazing on great snow-covered mountain tops, I know that all that wonder will be only like steps to what waits above for us.'

Faster Home

At Christmas, Fanny was sick again and the doctor insisted she must rest. But Fanny was cheerful and told him, 'I really have had such songs given me in the night, and some Christmas verses for next year came so easily.'

'But you must rest until you are strong enough for these things, Miss Frances,' the doctor said. As he left he nodded to Maria, 'Our patient does more good than I can do for her.'

An hour later, as Maria brought tea, Fanny's face was flushed with excitement. 'Oh, Maria; I've done half a day's work already. A whole set of mottoes has come to me; 'Christmas Sunshine,' and 'Love and light for the New Year.' What books I should love to write if I had time! I wonder if I will always be so busy with other things. But never mind, it is all service.'

'Yes, but you must not mind that now while you are supposed to be resting,' Maria said, as she handed Fanny her tea.

'Maria, do you remember our own mother's last words to me before she died?' Maria nodded as Fanny said, 'It's been the prayer of my life, "O Lord, prepare me for all you are preparing for me." I know he is.' Fanny sighed wearily. A moment later, with a note of cheerfulness on its way to becoming laughter, she added, 'I do hope the angels will have orders to let me rest a bit, when I first get to heaven!' Maria did laugh at the very thought of it!

Someone sent Fanny a little *Journal of Mercies* to keep a daily account of some mercy God had sent. And Fanny loved making orderly lists. The only hard part was choosing one special mercy to fit in the small space for each day. January, February and March included mercies like: able to come downstairs for the first time, a little rest from letter writing, and finally in late January, travelling opportunities to London! In March she wrote, 'finished writing my book *Kept*'. There were mercies for every date, and Fanny could have written a thousand more. She had just finished writing one, when Maria came into the study with a tea tray for them both.

Fanny's desk made Maria smile. 'I think you are just like our father was, so organised!' she said. 'You have a place for every single item; paper, clips, bits of string, everything!' Fanny's daily prayer list was on the desk next to her Bible, and it too was neatly divided into people and things to pray about for each day, morning and evening.

'Here is one list I want to show you, Maria.' Fanny said, holding it up. 'It's a list of work for this year, 1879: If the Lord will.' Fanny read the list to her:

'Write *Starlight through the Shadows*, a daily book for invalids. Six more Church Missionary Society papers. *Marching Orders*. Put *Loyal Responses* to music. Prepare

Kept for press. Write *Lilies from the Waters of Quietness,* a poem. Article, *About Bible Reading and Bible Marking, All Things,* work up my notes. *Particularly good to me,* verses or short article.' Fanny stopped reading for a moment and said, 'that one began with old Mr. Howell and his worn coat.' Maria smiled and nodded. 'Next,' Fanny read, 'I hope to write *The Stray Kitten* for children. Also work up C.S.S.M anecdotes into papers or a book. Complete twelve *Wayside Chimes* for *Home Words* magazine. Select or write *Echoes from the Word* for *Day of Days.* Write double sets of New Year's mottoes for Caswell's beautifully illustrated cards. Do *Bright Thoughts for Dark Days.* A series of Irish sketches for *Day of Days.* Work on *Sunday Postal Burdens* about how to relieve the postmen. *Our Brother,* or daily thoughts for those who love him. *Morning Stars*, daily thoughts about Jesus for little ones. *Evening Stars* or promises for the little ones. Complete the series of *Sunday Morning Crumbs* (texts to think about each Sunday). And Six poems for Sunday Magazine.'

'It's a wonderful list, a whole year's writing, if the Lord wills,' Maria said.

'And I am so glad to do whatever seems the Lord's will for me,' Fanny said. The post continued to bring piles of letters, many of them with requests for her help. Maria helped answer the ones she could. Fanny also loved visiting the cottages nearby, doing what she and Maria could to comfort the poor. Often someone would beg Fanny for a song, and she gladly sang songs she hoped would reach their hearts for Jesus. Sometimes, even here in their small village, Fanny saw lives broken and ruined through drunkenness, a widespread evil throughout England. She was soon volunteering to help with the Temperance Society's work to persuade men and boys to pledge themselves not to drink alcohol. To her joy, several lads in the village had signed the pledge to give up the drinking that called to them night after night in the pubs. The Bruey Branch, formed to collect for the work of the Irish Society, was growing too. And God was blessing her books! Fanny's heart was glad for the letters that came to tell her how he was using them in so many ways. 'Maria, it is really very remarkable how the Lord is blessing everything,' she said, as she continued working through the stack of mail.

Of all the things Fanny loved doing, reaching out to children brought her some of the greatest pleasure. Visiting the village school to speak with the children was one of them. 'Now, children,' she told them one morning as she finished a story, 'I have a surprise for you!' In her hand was a fine new Bible. 'I want to give a new Bible just like this to every child who learns to repeat the 53rd chapter of Isaiah.' A sea of hands went up to take on the project. The date fixed was Good Friday. Fanny was delighted with all those who repeated the chapter perfectly. The next lad, a stout little fellow named Michael, did well almost to the end of the chapter then stumbled trying to recall the next word.

When no amount of hard thinking brought it back to him, Fanny softly said, 'Michael, it might help if you try again a bit later. I am sure it will come to you. You are almost at the end and have done so well.' On Michael's next try he did it all nonstop and perfectly. With others, Fanny wisely arranged for a second day to try again. 'The gospel story is such glad news, I want you all to know it,' Fanny had told them. She loved bringing that good news to little children.

When the new book *Kept*, a book that took the lines of the song *Ever Only all for Thee* to talk about things like our voices, our minds, our hearts being kept for Jesus, was finished, Fanny went quickly to work on *Morning Stars* for little children.

She had just heard that her music for the words of a friend's song, *Loving All Along* was accepted for publication. It was one that the well-known American singer, Ira Sankey, wrote to say he could not get out of his mind. Fanny had heard Mr. Sankey sing at one of the D.L. Moody meetings in London, and when the Sankeys came to visit at Mumbles to ask if they might take the song to America, she was glad to send it. Mr. Sankey was also a close friend of the blind American song writer Fanny Crosby, whose songs Fanny loved, and Fanny sent along a poem she'd written for her. Its last stanza said:

Dear blind sister over the sea!
An English heart goes forth to thee.
We are linked by a cable of faith and song,
Flashing bright sympathy swift along;

> *One in the East and one in the West*
> *Singing for him who our souls love best,*
> *Singing for Jesus, telling His love*
> *All the way to our home above …*
> *Sister! What will our meeting be*
> *When our hearts shall sing and our eyes shall see!*

The post, with its stack of mail addressed to Miss Frances R. Havergal, had brought news from The Irish Society Fanny helped collect for. The Bruey Branch collections were so large that Fanny wrote back to say, 'I am alarmed how large the collections have been and don't know how I can keep pace with many new young collectors coming in. Hundreds of 'Bruey' cards are being taken all over the kingdom, and I see that the whole thing will need organising. Two years ago, I began with a list of eight collectors and have just sent in no less than seventy-nine collectors' lists and amounts. I am believing in prayer more than ever!'

In March, Fanny began planning a trip for the first week in June to Ireland with two of Ellen's sons, Willie and Alfred. She wrote to them:

> *Things are growing so fast in my department of the Irish*
> *Society, that I must go and see for myself what is being done*
> *in the fields and visit headquarters to see about organising*
> *the Bruey Branch. It is the land of your birth and I would*
> *love to take you to see some of the Irish stations …*
> *Your loving Aunt.*

It was early May, and a feverish cold had kept Fanny home. A new servant girl who'd come to serve at

Mumbles had asked to stay home from church in order
to be with Fanny. The two sat together in order to have
a little Bible study. 'Mary,' Fanny said, 'I love these times
together looking at his Word.'

Mary's round face had an earnest look as she said,
'It's so plain and clear the way you tell it, that it does
my own heart good!'

Fanny smiled and began to read to her the words of
John 8:51: 'Verily, verily, I say unto you, If a man keep
my saying, he shall never see death.' Oh how good that
makes my heart feel too, Mary.'

Fanny was better and this day she had promised
some men and boys to meet them in the village with
her temperance book for those who wanted to sign
it. True to their word, the men and boys were there
waiting for her to speak to them. 'Here we are and I
am so glad, though we could do with a bit of sunshine,'
Fanny began. There were smiles and laughter about
the weather and the heavy clouds coming up from the
sea channel. It was a cold spot to stand on, and sure
enough Fanny didn't make it home before rain and mist
chilled her through.

The next day was Ascension Day and there was to be
a service and communion at the little church. Fanny did
not look well and Maria was firm. 'If you are coming,
Fanny, you need only come for communion.'

'I will do that and I will even get a donkey ride
home.' Fanny promised. She was tired and did hire a
donkey. Like all donkeys for hire it came with a boy to

lead it. His name was Fred. As they passed through the village, some of the boys who knew of her temperance work came to hear what she was saying to Fred, and there was soon quite a gathering.

Fanny continued speaking, 'So you see, that you had better leave the devil's side and get on the safe side. Jesus Christ is the winning side! He loves and is calling us, won't you choose him for your Captain?' By the time they came to the house, Fred asked to sign the pledge. Fanny went inside for her temperance book, and Fred leaned it on the saddle and wrote his name in it. There was one more visit Fanny just had to make that evening.

A young sailor in the cottages was to report to his ship the very next day, and Fanny felt the need to see him this very night before he left. At the cottage she spoke loving words as the family listened. Afterwards, while tears filled the father's eyes and streamed down the mother's face, the young sailor signed Fanny's pledge book. Two of his little brothers, who had been in Fanny's class, eagerly watched their brother sign. As Fanny left the cottage she prayed for them and especially for the young sailor, 'Lord, go with him and let your Word fill his heart.'

The next day, Fanny continued to feel chilled as she sat in her study, near the fire. Piles of large temperance cards lay in her lap and on the small table at her side. Maria had just brought a cup of broth to her. 'The temperance meeting this evening will be very large, I think,' Fanny said.

Maria began to gather up the piles of cards and stacked them neatly together. 'The doctor said you must rest,' she said. 'I can take all these with me tonight.'

'I feel relieved, really, though I would have liked to be there, I am quite cheerful to be right here tonight. You will do so much better than I can, Maria. Oh, will you also take a message to the vicar and Mr. Bishop, sending my good wishes and request for bright, short addresses?'

Maria tucked a second wool shawl about Fanny's shoulders, chuckling as she did. 'Fanny, do pray that the vicar and his friend will be at least short.'

When Mary came to fetch the tea tray, Fanny was stitching strong paper tract-bags for sailors at sea. An hour later Mary came again to check on her, and saw at once how ill she looked. 'Here now, Miss Frances, let me help you to bed.' By the time Maria came home, Fanny lay tossing with fever.

As soon as she could sit up in bed, Fanny answered some of her letters, one of them on the back of her friend's own letter, when she could not reach other paper. Her note was brief and loving, but quickly ended with, 'Maria has just come and says I must not write anymore. Yours ever, F.R.H.'

The following day Fanny corrected a single proof of *Morning Stars* for children, on the text *I am the Bright and Morning Star*[1]. She finished, smiled faintly, and let Maria remove her pen, one she would not hold again.

---

1. Revelation 22:16

She was content to rest and enjoy her pet kittens, Trot and Dot, curled on the quilt near her feet. The doctor had just said she was not seriously ill, but must rest. 'And do you mind having to rest?' he asked.

Fanny smiled and said, 'I think of it the way an errand boy must when he is told to take a message, and then told by the master not to go after all. I was going to Ireland next week for the Irish Society, but God has upset all my plans, and it's all right.' The doctor simply nodded as he left.

It was Mary, the servant who loved Fanny reading to her, that came to read a text to Fanny, the last one Fanny would look at with her or anyone. 'It do say,' Mary read slowly, 'Be thou faithful unto death, and I will give thee a crown of life.'[2]

'How good,' Fanny said, 'that was the last text my papa ever read.'

Fever and pain and all the symptoms of peritonitis[3] came on rapidly, and Mary was one of those ready to do all she could to comfort her. Fanny, concerned for those around her, asked her sister, Miriam, to see that all who nursed her also took time to rest. Miriam seemed to be at her bedside always.

A letter came from her nephews, Willie and Ethelbert, which was the last letter she could listen to. 'Tell them I do hope my dear nephews will be

---

2. Revelation 2:10.
3. Peritonitis is an inflammation of the peritoneum, the thin tissue that lines the inner wall of the abdomen and covers most of the abdominal organs.

ambassadors for Christ; even if they are not clergymen, may they win souls,' Fanny said.

The doctors had done all they could, but nothing stopped the constant sickness or relieved her pain. Fanny tried to comfort the ones who cared for her and those who came to stay a moment with her, like her close friend Mrs. Morgan, the vicar's wife. To her she whispered, 'There is no bottom to God's mercy and love; all his promises are true. Not one thing has failed.' To the vicar she gave little messages: 'Tell the Y.W.C.A. all we spoke of him is true, and the Lord Jesus is a good, big foundation to rest on. And oh, how I want all of you to speak bright, bright words about Jesus, oh do. It's all perfect peace, I am only waiting for Jesus to take me in.'

Once, she asked Maria if it was wrong to groan when in such pain. 'I do want to glorify him, every step of the way.'

Maria told her how very, very patient she had been. 'Even the doctors have noticed it, and remarked on your calmness.'

The family had all come, and her brother Frank prayed for her and then he played and sang the songs she loved, like *Christ for me*.

One of the doctors needed to leave and bent over Fanny to say goodbye. 'I shall not see you again,' he said.

'Then do you really think I am going?' Fanny whispered.

'Yes,' the doctor replied.

'Today?'

'Probably,' he said.

'Beautiful, too good to be true!' Fanny whispered. A little while later, she smiled and said, 'Splendid to be so near the gates of heaven! So beautiful to go!' Frank had just finished singing *Jerusalem my happy home* and Fanny asked him to sing *How Sweet the Name of Jesus Sounds*.

The kindly vicar bent close to Fanny and said, 'You have talked and written so much about the King; and soon you will see him.'

Fanny whispered, 'I thought he might leave me here a long while; but he is so good to take me now.' And then she whispered, 'Come, Lord Jesus, come and take me.' And turning to Maria she asked, 'Do you think I shall be disappointed?'

'No, dearest, we are quite sure you are going to him now.'

At dawn, she slept a few moments and woke to say, 'I am lost in amazement! He has not failed one word of all his good promises!' After a moment, she whispered, 'Tell them to trust in Jesus.'

Softly, Ellen repeated the words, *Jesus, I will trust Thee*, and Fanny faintly sang the rest of the song with her:

Jesus, I will trust Thee,
Trust Thee with my soul
Guilty, lost, and helpless,
Thou hast made me whole:
There is none in heaven,
Or on earth, like Thee;

> Thou hast died for sinners,
> Therefore Lord for me.

One last convulsion racked Fanny's body as the nurse held her. Then, lying back on her pillows, Fanny folded her hands, saying, 'There, now it is all over! Blessed rest!' Her face seemed to light with joy and a single note of song came from her 'He'... a song not finished on earth. At last, she had stepped above the snow-topped mighty mountains to the glory she knew waited high above them.

Books would be written, filled with her poems and songs, her works spread throughout the British Empire and in many other countries. But it was in the heart of a lonely princess, the heart of a lost girl in a Swiss inn, the heart of a young sailor gone to sea and everywhere that Fanny planted the seed of the good news for Jesus that was her true legacy. *All for Jesus*, a song she wrote from her heart, was far more than a song, it was her life, the one he gave her to live for him on earth, and now she was home forever to live with the King.

Thinking Further Topics

1. Little Quicksilver

As a baby, it seemed that Fanny cooed in time to nursery lullabies her brother sang to her. She also wrote letters in rhyme and her first poem at the age of seven, followed by short stories. Like Fanny's gifts, do our gifts seem to be things we enjoy doing? What good things might you always have liked to do? Take a look back then discuss how these might be God's gifts to you. The Bible tells us that all of us receive gifts of various kinds. (See James 1:17) Read 1 Corinthians 12:4-11 – how do we know that every one of us receives a gift? Talk about ways to use these various gifts for the Lord Jesus. Do you think he has a place to use yours?

2. The Terrible Sermon

How did Mr. Philpotts' powerful sermon on hell, affect Fanny's life? What was her new picture of God? Do you ever think of God as angry? How does God see us when we turn to Jesus and trust him with our lives? (See 1 John 3:1). What does the Bible say about hell? (See Rev. 20:15). How can we know we are not going to hell? (See John 3:16-18). The visiting pastor didn't help Fanny when she talked to him; what could he have said to help her? Do you know people like that pastor? If so, talk about where you and others can find those you know could help.

3. 'I Fear You Are Not Prepared'

When Fanny's mother said, 'Pray to God to prepare you for all that he is preparing for you,' how were her words true for Fanny at that time? What did Fanny do with her terrible sorrow over her mother's death? Fanny told Ellen on the night before she left school, 'I can't love God yet.' Have you ever felt this way? Did this mean God didn't have any more part in Fanny's life? From reading about her life, do you think God was actually at work even then in her life? Can you think of times God was working to bring things about for your good, even when you might not have known it? Talk about God's faithfulness to us even when we may be unfaithful. (See 2 Tim. 2:13).

4. Can You Trust Jesus?

At boarding school, Fanny found friends and learned something more about being a Christian. What amazed Fanny when her classmate Diana said all this time she hadn't been a Christian up till now? What happened to Diana to change her? How did her motives and desires change? Why do our motives and desires matter? What do you think was missing from Fanny's nightly prayers to become a Christian?

When Miss Cooke asked Fanny why she couldn't trust Jesus to save her, what suddenly happened to Fanny? Talk about the difference between knowing or believing something is true, and trusting. Talk about when one asks Jesus to save them, what do we trust him to do? How did Fanny take that step into trusting Jesus? Talk about how we can know we have been saved. (See 1 John 1:9 and John 20:31). Can you think of other promises like these?

5. 'You Must Not Go Back to School'

What was Fanny's reaction to being told she could not go back to school? In a letter to Elizabeth, she said she had started school prayerfully and ended up wanting to surpass others in everything. She called it her besetting sin, pride. Not going to school made her disappointed and impatient, but it was a time meant to teach her something she needed to learn. Talk about pride and how you think it can become a sin in a person's life. How can spending time alone thinking about the things God wants for us help? Are there puzzling times in your life, where God might be using them for your good? Talk about Jeremiah 29:11 and how it applies to our lives.

6. Alone in a Hard Place

What was the 'cost' of living the way a Christian should at Fanny's German boarding school, where she was the only Christian? Is there any cost like that at your school or even in your family life? What did Jesus say about the cost of following him? (See John 16:33). What does 1 Peter 3:14-17 say we can do in these situations? Do we always see the reward of doing the right thing? What does the Bible say about rewards? (See Matt. 10:32,42 and Matt. 6:19-20).

7. Mission to Ireland

What effect did Fanny's singing and speaking have on some of the Irish girls in Ellen's Bible study? Can you think of a time when someone had that kind of effect on you? If God could use a time like Fanny's concert for these girls to bring one of them closer to himself, is it possible that he might use special events at our church to bring someone to him? How can we help? Talk about how young people might carry out Jesus' command in Matthew 28:19-20.

8. The New Governess

When the great composer Mr. Hiller says that Fanny does have enough musical talent to make a career of music, Fanny tells Elizabeth that she wants to serve the Lord in any way he plans for her. She believes more and more that she will be singing for him and witnessing where she can. She could have served God through a musical career and said she might someday develop her talent, but what do you see as the key thing here that her choices will be made on? Talk about, 'Serving the Lord in any way he plans for me.' Does he have a plan for each of us? (See Jeremiah 29:11). How do you think Fanny felt 'more and more convinced of what she is to do?'

9. The Mountains of her Dreams

Fanny had dreamt of seeing snow mountains, and finds them just as pure and bright and peaceful as she dreamt them. She imagined them rising out of the earth to soaring heights as if they were the first glimpse of the great unseen heavenly city above them. God uses mountains in Scripture to tell us about himself. See Psalm 121:1-2 and Psalm 125: 1-2. Talk about how God's might and glory are seen in creation. (See Romans 1:20).

Fanny also spoke about Jesus to a maid at the first inn they stayed, and later to a Jewish man and his daughter on a boat ride. Afterwards, she wrote in her journal, 'Tell them what you know is true; tell them what he is to you.' Is this a good way to witness for the Lord? Talk about some truths you could tell another person in witnessing. Why is it important to know what he is to you?

10. The Queen is Pleased

Fanny dedicated her book of *Sacred Songs* to the young Princess Beatrice, a lonely secluded girl. In one song, *Evening Prayer*, she wrote of Jesus, the friend, she wanted the princess and all children to know. Fanny loved bringing the good news of Jesus to children and wrote much for them. Jesus had some things to say about children. (See Matthew 19:14). Talk about reaching children for Jesus. Did Jesus command this or merely suggest we not hinder children from coming to him? Talk about ways your church reaches out to the children. How might we help or hinder? Fanny asked the Lord to take the gift of writing she had, however small, to make it for his use. Can even a story for children be one of those small gifts he can use? Can you think of a Christian book or story that once helped you?

11. A Sudden Sorrow

The death of Fanny's father was a great loss to her, leaving her truly an orphan. When she was really missing his help with her work on a hymn, she remembered Psalm 27:10, God's promise to orphans. Talk about how a promise like this one can help when we lose a parent. Does God know when we are sad? (See Exodus 3:7). Earlier, Fanny said our heart's cry is like a wordless prayer to God. Think about Isaiah 53:4 – was our sorrow one of the things Jesus took on himself? What does Jesus want us to do with our cares or anxieties or sorrows? (See 1 Peter 5:7).

When Fanny's stepmother began to make her wishes known about Fanny's work on the *Havergal Psalmody*, Fanny really wanted to do something better for her own future. What sacrifice did she make? What did she ask her friends to pray about her attitude towards making that sacrifice? Can you think of times when you have faced doing something your own way or choosing to sacrifice your way for someone else's good? How would our attitude about not having our way matter? Talk about how praying for one another helps most when we honestly admit what it is we need prayer for. (See Hebrews 4:15-16).

12. In the Alps Again!

When Fanny and Elizabeth travelled through France to Switzerland they came through many war-ravaged places in France. As they handed out tracts and booklets people welcomed them. Why do you think wounded soldiers and widows and so many others were so glad to take these Bible tracts? How are Christians reaching out to suffering people today?

What happened when one tourist left behind a New Testament with one of Fanny and Elizabeth's guides? Fanny and Elizabeth didn't always see the results of the seeds they were spreading everywhere. What does Jesus says about this in John 4:37-38?

13. Full Surrender

Fanny loved to serve the Lord Jesus, though illness or things beyond her control often kept her from it. Sometimes she felt like everyone else was doing better than herself and it made her feel down. When Fanny read a book called *All For Jesus,* it changed her life. She said, 'I know I love Jesus and love to serve him, but all for Jesus means so much more.' It meant a full surrender of her life to Jesus! Why do you think simply giving herself to Jesus and trusting him to keep her, made her feel that at last she was standing in the sunlight? (See Jude 1:24-25). Talk about her hymn *Ever Only all For Thee,* and think how it might apply to your life at home, at school, or anywhere. How do you know that God will keep on working in our lives when we give them over to him? (See Philippians 1:6).

14. 'Kept'

On her third trip to the Alps, Fanny lost her way and found herself forced to stay at a small isolated mountain inn. Here she faced the worst situation in all the Swiss inns she had ever visited. How did God use her meeting with an angry, rude young serving girl? It could have made Fanny fearful to be in the situation she was. Instead, that night, she prayed for the girl and asked God to do what two specific things for herself and the girl? What did Fanny say to this girl the next day? Talk about the simple thing Fanny said first to the girl. Why do you think it was a good approach? Does God sometimes allow us to end up in a place we would rather not be, or put someone in our lives like the angry Swiss girl? How did the girl respond to Fanny's gift of the little booklet? What can we learn from this incident?

Fanny left, still praying for the girl, and sometimes we too can only do that as we move on. Is there any place in the world where God cannot find us? (See Psalm 139).

15. God's Half-Timer

In her times of illness, when all Fanny could do was wait for whatever Jesus would choose for her, she found out that waiting for him, was also waiting with him, and that made all the difference. (See 1 Peter 5:7 and the second part of Hebrews 13:5, also verse 6). Talk about times when you or someone close to you had to take time out and wait and see. What do you think waiting for him means? What about waiting with him?

When Fanny could only do a half-day's work she said Jesus can make a half-hour's work worth a whole day's if he wills. She couldn't be a missionary in India, but her books and songs went for her, and letters came to tell her how God was using them. What makes the difference in whatever we do to serve the Lord, whether it's a little thing we can do that may not seem important? Look at John 15:1-2 for what Jesus says about us being like branches. Who is the vine-keeper? Why is he pruning the vine (us)?

Fanny tells about a vine-keeper who worked patiently for fourteen years to bring one vine's branch to bear very good fruit. When we can't see what God is doing in our lives, what must we do? What did you think of Fanny's illustration of how God's words can be like little pillows to rest our hearts on?

16. Faster Home

When Fanny was near death, the vicar said, 'You have written and talked so much about the King and soon you will see him. Five of her books were called 'The

Royal Series', beginning with the first one *My King*. Perhaps you have never thought much about Jesus being a real King.

Is Jesus a King? Why did the wise men think he was a King? (See Matthew 2:1-2). What does God, the Father, say about Jesus being King? (See Hebrews 1:8).

Who does Jesus the King reign over? (See Philippians 2:9-11).

How much power and authority does he have? (See Matthew 28:18).

Jesus said that heaven and earth may pass away, but his Word will never pass away. (See Matthew 24:35). How would you explain to someone that Jesus is a true King?

Fanny wanted everyone to trust Jesus, and before she died she said, 'I am lost in amazement! He has not failed one word of all his good promises!' Talk about the last song Fanny sang with Ellen,

Jesus, I will trust Thee,
Trust thee with my soul
Guilty, lost, and helpless,
Thou hast made me whole:
There is none in heaven,
Or on earth, like Thee;
Thou hast died for sinners,
Therefore Lord for me.

How is this the gospel that makes us ready to die, ready to see our King?

Frances Ridley Havergal Timeline

1836	Born 14th December, at Astley Rectory, Worcestershire, U.K., youngest of the six children of William and Jane Havergal; siblings: Jane Miriam [Crane] (19 at the time of FRH's birth), Henry (16), Maria (15), Ellen [Shaw] (13), Francis (7).
1838	Coronation of Queen Victoria. Invention of the electric telegraph.
1836-1842	Lived in Astley, where her father was the Church of England rector.
1842-1845	Temporary home at Henwick House, Hallow, Worcestershire.
1845-1860	Lived in the Rectory of St. Nicholas in the city of Worcester.
1848	Her mother died on 5th July.
1851	Her father married Caroline Cooke.
1850-1851	Attended the Belmont School for Girls, London. Passenger railway service arrived in Worcester in 1850.
1852-1853	First visit to Germany, attended the Luisenschule in Düsseldorf.
1854	Fanny confirmed in the Church of England, at Worcester Cathedral on 17th July.

1856	First trip to Ireland.
1859	Wrote *I Gave My Life for Thee*, her first published hymn.
1861-1867	Oakhampton House (in Dunley, near Astley), governess to the two youngest daughters of her oldest sister, Jane Miriam Crane.
1867	First trip to Switzerland; followed by four more trips: 1871, 1873, 1874, 1876. Atlantic Ocean cable communication installed.
1869	First book published, *The Ministry of Song*.
1867-1870	Stayed with her father and stepmother in Leamington, Worcestershire; joined the Y.W.C.A. Invention of the first commercially successful typewriter, 1868.
1870	Published *Sacred Songs for Little Singers*.
1870	Fanny's father dies, on 19th April.
1871	*Havergal's Psalmody* published.
1871	Continues to live with her stepmother in Leamington.
1874	Published her most well-known hymn, *Take My Life and Let it Be*.
1878	Stepmother's death in May.
1878	October, moved to Mumbles, Wales where she spent the remaining months of her life with her sister Maria.
1879	Fanny dies on 3rd June.

Bibliography

Crane, J. Miriam, editor, *Swiss Letters and Alpine Poems by the Late Frances Ridley Harvegal*. London: James Nisbet & Co., 1881.

Bly, Tacey, compiler, *Frances Ridley Havergal: The Poems and Hymns of Christ's Sweet Singer*. New Canaan, CT: Keats Publishing Inc., 1977.

Bugden, Pamela D., *Ever, only, All for Thee: Frances Ridley Havergal. Glimpses of Her Life and Writings*. Hannibal, MO: Granted Ministries Press, 2009.

Bullock, Charles, *The Sisters: Frances Ridley Havergal. Maria V. G. Havergal*. London: "Home Words" Publishing House, [1890?].

Davies, Rev. E., *Frances Ridley Havergal: A Full Sketch of Her Life, with Choice Selections from her Prose and Poetical Writings*. Reading, MA: Holiness Book Concern, 1884.

Enock, Esther E., *Frances Ridley Havergal*. London: Pickering and Inglis, 1936.

Havergal, Frances Ridley, *Children's Devotions: for morning and evening*. Scotland: Christian Focus Publications, 2004.

Havergal, Frances Ridley, *Under the Surface*. London: J. Nisbet & Co., 1882.

Havergal, Maria V. G., *Memorials of Frances Ridley Havergal*. New York: Anson D. R. Randolph Co., 1880.

Havergal, Maria V. G., editor, *The Poetical Works of Frances Ridley Havergal*. New York: E. P. Dutton & Co., 1896.

Author's Note

Though Frances Ridley Havergal began writing for print in the mid-1850s, most of her published works appeared in the final ten years of her life, and some, like *Kept for the Master's Use*, were published posthumously. Her output included poems, books, children's books, devotional works, articles for magazines, penny books, and leaflets. Frances wrote hundreds of poems, hymns and dozens of hymn tunes. Some that are still used in our churches today are:

- I Gave My Life for Thee
- Lord, Speak to Me that I May Speak
- Take My Life and Let it Be (also known as the 'Consecration Hymn')
- I Am Trusting Thee, Lord Jesus
- Like A River Glorious
- Who is On the Lord's Side?
- True-Hearted, Whole-Hearted

Old Recipe for Apple Turnover

Slice off enough lard to fill a ⅓ measuring cup, separating the fat from stringy parts (today we actually have a great lard for this called Leaf Lard and also Pork Suet).

Rub it into the flour and salt and bring the dough together with some cold water. (No measurements in this part, but probably 5 cups flour).

Roll out dough, slice in squares, put dollop of apples (again no measurement here, but probably 4 Granny type apples peeled, cored and sliced) mixed with cinnamon and brown sugar, probably about 1 teaspoon cinnamon and 1 cup brown sugar). Place apple mix in centre of each square.

Fold dough over the apples to make a triangle and seal edges (press with fingers all around edge).

Bake in hot oven (probably 375-400°F) for 30 minutes. One can also fry them instead of baking.

Easy Recipe for Apple Turnover

Pastry
1 cup (125g) flour
½ teaspoon salt
⅓ cup (75g) butter
⅜ cup (85g) cream cheese
Mix and make into 4-6 little balls
Chill.

Filling
1½ cups (262g) chopped apples (fine), ¼ cup (56g) sugar, ¼ teaspoon cinnamon, dash of nutmeg. Mix together. Spoon into rolled dough to make individual turnovers. Seal edges with fork.

Bake at 400°F (200°C) for 20 minutes. Sprinkle with powdered sugar.

If I were trying to make original Astley apple turnovers, I would guess she also added a good sprinkle of nutmeg along with cinnamon. And she probably sprinkled them with a bit of sugar when baked. (I always add both nutmeg and cinnamon to apple pie).

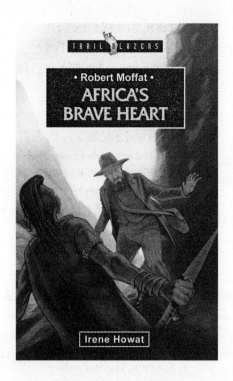

Robert Moffat, Africa's Brave Heart
by Irene Howat
ISBN 978-1-84550-715-2

The story of a Scottish minister and his wife in Africa – the precursors to David Livingstone. With a sword, a shovel, a Bible, and great courage, Robert used the skills he had learned growing up in a Scottish village to translate the Bible into Tswana and to share God's love with Africa.

OTHER BOOKS IN THE
TRAILBLAZER SERIES

Augustine, The Truth Seeker
ISBN 978-1-78191-296-6
David Brainerd, A Love for the Lost
ISBN 978-1-84550-695-7
Paul Brand, The Shoes that Love Made
ISBN 978-1-84550-630-8
John Bunyan, The Journey of a Pilgrim
ISBN 978-1-84550-458-8
John Calvin, After Darkness Light
ISBN 978-1-84550-084-9
Fanny Crosby, The Blind Girl's Song
ISBN 978-1-78191-163-1
Billy Graham, Just Get Up Out Of Your Seat
ISBN 978-1-84550-095-5
John Knox, The Sharpened Sword
ISBN 978-1-78191-057-3
C.S. Lewis, The Storyteller
ISBN 978-1-85792-487-9
Eric Liddell, Finish the Race
ISBN 978-1-84550-590-5
Robert Moffat, Africa's Brave Heart
ISBN 978-1-84550-715-2
John Newton, A Slave Set Free
ISBN 978-1-78191-350-5
Mary of Orange, At the Mercy of Kings
ISBN 978-1-84550-818-0
John Stott, The Humble Leader
ISBN 978-1-84550-787-9

CHRISTIAN FOCUS PUBLICATIONS

Christian Focus | Christian Heritage | CF4K | Mentor

Christian Focus Publications publishes books for adults and children under its four main imprints: Christian Focus, CF4K, Mentor and Christian Heritage. Our books reflect our conviction that God's Word is reliable and Jesus is the way to know him, and live for ever with him.

Our children's publication list includes a Sunday School curriculum that covers pre-school to early teens, and puzzle and activity books. We also publish personal and family devotional titles, biographies and inspirational stories that children will love.

If you are looking for quality Bible teaching for children then we have an excellent range of Bible stories and age-specific theological books.

From pre-school board books to teenage apologetics, we have it covered!

Find us at our web page:
www.christianfocus.com

CF4•K
Because you're never
too young to know Jesus